Petroleum and Mexico's Future

Letter from the Americas Society President

The Americas Society is a nonprofit, private institution established in 1981 to coordinate the activities of various U.S. organizations dealing with hemispheric affairs, including matters relevant to Mexico, Central and South America, the Caribbean, and Canada. The Society, which is national in scope, is located in New York City, with affiliates in New York and Washington, including the Center for Inter-American Relations, the Council of the Americas, the Pan American Society of the United States, and Caribbean/Central American Action.

Among the objectives of the Americas Society is to provide a forum for the discussion of issues vital to the hemisphere and to improve understanding of the economic, political, and cultural values of all countries of the Americas. The Americas Society seeks to provide a forum through which leaders from government, business, academia, the media, the arts, politics, and other areas can make their thoughts known to diverse national and international audiences.

It is our hope that this book, along with previous and forthcoming volumes sponsored by the Americas Society and its affiliates, will contribute significantly to the research and commentary on this subject.

—Ambassador George W. Landau

About the Book and Editor

Addressing the effects of the 1982 crisis, through the late 1980s, on Mexico's economic and political systems and assessing the country's potential for entering a period of strong economic growth, contributors to this volume focus on oil, the primary source of Mexico's foreign exchange earnings, and on trade with the United States, the primary means for earning foreign exchange. The authors argue that the problems Mexico faced during the crisis period are not over; indeed, the most difficult challenges lie ahead. For the remainder of the century Mexico must earn adequate revenue to service a substantial debt and to permit the economy to grow at a rate that provides opportunity for a labor force already enduring a high rate of unemployment and rising inflation. Contributors agree that the key to Mexico's economic and political stability will be the control of inflation, unemployment, and large public-sector deficits.

Pamela S. Falk is associate director of the Institute of Latin American and Iberian Studies at Columbia University, where she teaches international relations. Professor Falk was formerly the director of the Americas Society's "Mexico Focus" project and director of Latin American Affairs at the Americas Society, Inc./Center for Inter-American Relations. She is a member of the Council on Foreign Relations and is on the board of directors of the Caribbean Cultural Center. Her books include *The Political Status of Puerto Rico* (editor) and *Cuban Foreign Policy: Caribbean Tempest.*

Published in cooperation
with the Americas Society, Inc.

Petroleum and Mexico's Future

edited by
Pamela S. Falk

Taylor & Francis Group

LONDON AND NEW YORK

First published 1987 by Westview Press, Inc.

Published 2019 by Routledge
52 Vanderbilt Avenue, New York, NY 10017
2 Park Square, Milton Park, Abingdon, Oxon OX14 4RN

Routledge is an imprint of the Taylor & Francis Group, an informa business

Library of Congress Cataloging-in-Publication Data
Petroleum and Mexico's future.
  (Westview special studies on Latin America and the
Caribbean)
  Bibliography: p.
  Includes index.
  1. Petroleum industry and trade—Mexico. 2. Mexico—
Economic conditions—1970. 3. Debts, External—Mexico.
4. Labor supply—Mexico. I. Falk, Pamela S. II. Series.
HD9574.M6P47 1987   338.2′7282′0972   86-13128

ISBN 13: 978-0-367-28280-6 (hbk)
ISBN 13: 978-0-367-29826-5 (pbk)

Contents

List of Tables ix

Foreword: Mexico's Economic and Political Future,
  Russell E. Marks, Jr. xi

Acknowledgments xiii

Introduction: Mexico's Political Economy—Oil and
  the Costs of Development, *Pamela S. Falk* 1

Part One
The Political Economy of Oil: Mexico's Debt
in the 1980s

1   Mexico: Is There Life After Debt? *Alan J. Stoga* 9

2   The Impact of the Debt Crisis on the Mexican
    Political System, *Susan Kaufman Purcell* 26

Part Two
The Impact of Trade on Mexico's Economy

3   U.S.-Mexico Trade Relations, *Guy F. Erb* 37

4   Mexico's Entrance into the General Agreement
    on Tariffs and Trade, *Alfredo Gutierrez Kirchner* 55

Part Three
The Implications of an Oil Economy: Benefits,
Stakes, and "Petrodependency"

5   The Role of the Oil Industry in Mexico,
    The Honorable Mario Ramón Beteta 63

6   Mexico: Petroleum Stakes and Risks in a Turbulent
    Marketplace, *Edward L. Morse* 82

7   The International Economic Crisis and the Battle for the Nation, *René Villarreal (translated by Edith Grossman)*.. 87

Appendixes

A   PEMEX Financial Statistics................................ 99

B   Inter-American Development Bank, *External Debt and Economic Development in Latin America*.................. 101

C   Morgan Guaranty Trust Company, *World Financial Markets*... 105

D   Petróleos Mexicanos, *PEMEX Information Bulletin, 1986–1990: Petroleum Prices and Projections*................ 106

Selected Bibliography: Mexico's Economic and Political Development, *Gabrielle S. Brussel*........................ 107

About the Editor and Contributors 116

Index... 120

Tables

1.1 Mexico: Growth and Inflation............................ 11

1.2 Mexico: Balance of Payments 13

1.3 Mexico: Debt and Debt Service........................... 18

Foreword:
Mexico's Economic
and Political Future

The Center for Inter-American Relations, an affiliate of the Americas Society, in 1984 gathered a group of distinguished Mexican and U.S. businesspeople and policymakers to discuss "Petroleum and Mexico's Future," the beginning of a project on the political impact of Mexico's economy that has culminated with the publication of this book.

When the conference was held, Mexico had already passed through the first shock of illiquidity late in 1982. A unique financial rescue package had been provided by a consortium, including agencies of the U.S. government, international lending institutions, and private commercial banks, to ensure the continued service of the foreign debt. Mexico had also agreed to adjust domestic economic practices to conform with International Monetary Fund guidelines designed to limit inflation. In 1983, as a direct result of the "austerity" measures in the domestic economy and the facilitation of exports, the country had once again generated an export surplus large enough to cover debt service.

The Mexican example of close cooperation with lending institutions and rapid implementation of domestic economic adjustment programs established a precedent for the other debtor countries of Latin America as they confronted similar crises. As our conferees were careful to point out, however, the Mexican recovery was dependent upon petroleum exports. The current export of 1.5 million barrels per day provides about 75 percent of Mexico's export earnings. Therefore, the precipitous decline in petroleum prices that commenced in 1985 may once again jeopardize foreign debt service. It could also have a devastating effect upon domestic economic development programs and, indeed, cause political instability. In fact, the continuing erosion of petroleum prices has increased the pertinence and confirmed the perspicacity of the work included in this book.

Russell E. Marks, Jr.
Senior Vice President, Haley Associates, Inc.
Former President, Americas Society, Inc.

Acknowledgments

Mexico's oil is a bedeviling subject for policymakers who have to shape policy based on it and for analysts who seek to understand the vicissitudes of the market. Keeping abreast of the dramatic changes in the price of petroleum and the consequent policy changes was difficult and demanding, and necessitated many updates to the manuscript. Accordingly, the Americas Society/Center for Inter-American Relations is enormously grateful to the Mexican government officials and the U.S. and Mexican industry analysts and contributors who displayed such willingness to update their manuscripts as new events required it.

The Mexican oil industry, Petróleos Mexicanos (PEMEX), was able to provide us with updated projections and examinations of the changes in the price of crude oil as well as of the impact those changes would have on Mexico's development plan and the Mexican economy in general. The result is an anthology that is both up to date and far reaching in its analysis. For this, we are grateful to the staff of PEMEX, particularly Mercedes Mazón, and to the New York and Washington regional director, Alfredo Gutierrez Kirchner.

Because the project involved both a conference and a book, several staff members of the Americas Society were instrumental in its completion. Special thanks go to Russell E. Marks, Jr., the former president, under whose direction the program took place, and to James DeNivo and Maricela Crespi for many of the finances related to both the conference and publication of the book. The conference itself would not have taken place without the competent assistance of Marion Sullivan, Beatrice Wolfe, Octavio Velázquez, and Mackey Browne.

Special help was given to this and other conferences by Albert Minero, the Americas Society theater director. Several student interns gave able assistance to research on the subject, including Stephen Gaull and Virginia Cutchin. And for skillful coordination of these publications, I thank John W. Dwyer, the director of Latin American Public Affairs.

For her skillful editing and her arduous devotion to reading, writing, and research, a very special debt is owed to Gabrielle Brussel, who went on to graduate work at Columbia University and served as senior research associate on this book and on the "Mexico Focus" project. Finally, I thank my colleagues at Columbia University's School of International and Public Affairs and its dean, Alfred C. Stepan, for their insights into Mexican affairs.

Without the contribution of the Tinker Foundation and its chairman and president, Martha Muse, the meeting with Lic. Mario Ramón Beteta, PEMEX's director general, would not have occurred. Several student interns minded every detail from displaying the Mexican flag to supervising the audiovisual mechanics of the conference, all of which was coordinated without a flaw by the administrative coordinator, Lauretta Cohen. Thanks also go to Anne C. Kubisch for her wise counsel in the early stages of the book's publication.

We are particularly grateful to Espinosa Iglesias and the Fundación Amparo R. de Espinosa Yglesias for their permission to use the painting by Diego Rivera for the jacket design of this book. They have been kind enough to allow access to many visitors into the Mexican room of the Americas Society headquarters in New York, at 680 Park Avenue, to enjoy the unusual beauty of this 1912 painting. The painting is on permanent loan to the Americas Society.

Westview Press has devoted time and expertise to the production of the book. We especially thank Barbara Ellington, Bruce Kellison, Libby Barstow, and Christine Arden for their effort to apply their high standards to the publication and promotion of this book.

Pamela S. Falk

Petroleum and Mexico's Future

Introduction:
Mexico's Political Economy—
Oil and the Costs of Development

Pamela S. Falk

"Bandera y petróleo" (the flag and oil) is a Mexican description of nationalism, and few adages better convey the central role of petroleum in Mexico's political economy. Although discussions of Mexico's economic woes center on inflation and unemployment, oil prices and oil production, interest rates and a depreciating currency, foreign investment and a declining trade surplus, and a growing budget deficit, both Mexican presidents since the 1982 financial crisis have argued that Mexico's strategy must take political realities into account. Strict economic calculations, according to that definition, do not include the impact of austerity programs on the Mexican population and thus on political stability. Growth, development, and distribution, the Mexican government argues, must remain central to Mexico's development plans.

Ever since the charismatic and popular General Lázaro Cárdenas nationalized the oil industry on March 18, 1938, Mexican development programs and their core—oil—have been "wrapped in the flag." At the time, with great reason to fear retaliation from both Europe and the United States, Mexico rallied the politicians, the people, and even the Church (in the name of the new archbishop, Luís Martínez) behind a new definition of "economic sovereignty" that would lead Mexico toward financial independence.

Curiously, the effort in 1938 was to regain Mexico's national resources and free the nation of foreign economic influences, particularly that of the United States. Writing of Mexico's relationship with its northern neighbor, Octavio Paz, the Mexican author and poet, observed that "ever since Mexicans began to be aware of a national identity—in about the middle of the eighteenth century—we have been interested in our neighbors. First, there was a mixture of curiousity and disdain; later an admiration and enthusiasm that were soon tinged with fear and envy."[1]

Mexico has, of course, grown by leaps and bounds in all areas since that time. In the subsequent three decades, Mexico's gross national product (GNP) grew by 6 percent annually, the population grew enormously, a rural majority moved to the cities, and the production of oil became central to Mexico's exports, hitting a high of 80 percent in 1982.

As Mario Ramón Beteta, former head of Mexico's national oil conglomerate, Petróleos Mexicanos (PEMEX), stated, Mexico's national oil wealth should, in theory, bring Mexico "beyond the reach of the ambitions of the powerful." But has it?

The benefits of Mexico's main revenue source—oil—have been questionable. Since prices reached a decade high of almost $40 a barrel in 1981, Mexico's crude slumped to less than $10 a barrel in April 1986, for the first time in a decade. Three months later, the international financial institutions and commercial banks, in negotiating the rescheduling of Mexico's debt, linked oil prices with Mexico's debt repayment schedule, a precedent established only in 1982. During 1986, Mexicans faced a deficit in their federal budget of 12 percent of gross domestic product (GDP), up from 9.6 percent in 1985. More significant, hopes that the program would halve the 1985 deficit to 4.9 percent in 1986 were dashed. Further eroding Mexico's economy was an inflation rate of 59 percent in 1984, 64 percent in 1985, and a projected 75 percent in 1986.

Consequently, instead of achieving its economic dream, Mexico's standard of living has been reduced by 30 percent since the 1982 crisis. Even so, the government pays 46 percent of its 1986 budget to debt servicing. Furthermore, neither international economic shifts nor nature itself have been kind to Mexico in recent years. The government plans to spend more than $4 billion between 1986 and 1989 for reconstruction following the devastation that occurred during Mexico's 1985 earthquake. High interest rates and low oil prices account for the largest part of Mexico's woes.

Finally, the subject of Mexico-U.S. trade continues to be high on the bilateral agenda. Indeed, the United States has been Mexico's main supplier and main customer, purchasing 61 percent of Mexican exports and supplying 66 percent of Mexico's imports in 1985, partly as a function of the first bilateral agreement signed between Mexico City and Washington since World War II.

As the second half of the decade continues, Mexico's economy is showing signs of both strength and strain. In 1984 and 1985, the economy reversed itself and began to grow, first by 3.7 percent and then by 2.7 percent, following two years of negative indicators. With Mexico's 1986 accession to the General Agreement on Tariffs and Trade (GATT), Mexico has moved toward a "liberalization" of its protected trade history, a change welcomed by its major trading partners. Innovative solutions to reduce the $98 billion dollar debt, including "debt-for-equity swaps" and "debt relief" involving commercial bank "write-downs" of portions of the foreign debt, have given Mexico's planners some room in which to move.

Yet signs of strain prevail. A 1986 poll revealed that more than 50 percent of all Mexicans believe that the economy is so mortally wounded that it will never survive. The flight of capital continued well into the late 1980s, with estimates ranging between $35 and $60 billion in "la fuga" (the exodus of Mexican money from the country) and only the promise of an improved investment climate to invite it back to Mexico.

And where does petroleum fit into the economic future of the nation? In 1986, oil lost $7 billion in revenue and the severe drop in oil prices took its toll on PEMEX surpluses, doubling the projected public-sector deficit to 10 percent of gross domestic project.

* * *

What are the implications for Mexico's future? Does Mexico's political system show signs of strain? How will this U.S. trading partner and neighbor fare in the future?

Focusing on the issues of oil, trade, and development, the contributors to this anthology address the effects of the crisis in the late 1980s on Mexico's economic and political systems and discuss the country's potential to repay its over $100 billion foreign debt. For the remainder of the century, the authors agree, Mexico must bring in sufficient revenue to service a substantial debt, cut back on the public-sector deficit, and privatize several government-owned industries.

The political impact of Mexico's oil economy is reviewed in Part One of this volume. Alan Stoga, a Kissinger Associates adviser with a background in commercial banking and in the U.S. Treasury Department, gives a history of the crisis in which he describes seven constraints in the Mexican economy. "Without a renewed commitment to thoroughgoing economic change," he warns, "and *probably* without increased availability of foreign capital, Mexico may be condemned to stagflation . . . or to a stop-go pattern of economic growth and decline." Susan Kaufman Purcell, director of the Latin American Project of the Council on Foreign Relations and former member of the U.S. State Department's Policy Planning Staff, analyzes the political implications of the continuing economic strains and examines Mexico's "most pressing problem," unemployment—a problem she projects is not likely to be solved in the foreseeable future.

Part Two follows with a discussion of the impact of trade on Mexico's economy. Included in this context are analyses by oil industry analyst and former National Security Council member Guy F. Erb and by Alfredo Gutierrez Kirchner, PEMEX's New York and Washington regional director.

Part Three follows with a discussion of the implications of the role that trade plays in the Mexican economy. With Mexico's 1986 accession to the General Agreement on Tariffs and Trade (GATT), Mexico's trade relations with the West have become an issue of central concern.

Featured in Part Three is a chapter by former director general of the petroleum industry of Mexico, the Honorable Mario Ramón Beteta. "We are concerned," he states, "about our contribution to energy independence, to economic independence, and to the political independence of our country." His analysis is both statistical and theoretical in its evaluation of an industry that, under his direction, has accounted for over two-thirds of Mexico's export earnings. Indeed, as Beteta points out, "The petroleum industry has taken on not only economic importance but political importance as well."

In the following chapter, Edward Morse, managing director of the Petroleum Finance Company and former deputy assistant secretary of state for Energy Policy, discusses the risks and stakes involved in reliance on the petroleum industry. After that, a comprehensive view of the benefits and costs of "petrodependency" is provided by René Villarreal, special adviser to the president of Mexico, Miguel de la Madrid, and official of the Ministry of Energy, Mining, and Parastatal Industry.

The consensus is that Mexico is both oil rich (and dependent) and cash poor, with a political system that is showing signs of real strain. The economic problems currently besetting Mexico—persistent inflation, a devalued currency, high unemployment, and an angry and growing political opposition to the government—are unfortunately likely to bedevil Mexico for years to come.

Notes

1. Octavio Paz, "Mexico and the United States: Positions and Counterpositions," in Tommie Sue Montgomery, ed., *Mexico Today* (Philadelphia, Pa.: Institute for the Study of Human Issues/Center for Inter-American Relations, 1982, p. 3.

References

Balassa, Bela; Bueno, Gerardo M.; Kuczynski, Pedro-Pablo; and Simonson, Mario Henrique. *Toward Renewed Economic Growth in Latin America.* Washington, D.C.: Institute for International Economics, 1986.

Berg, Eric N. "U.S. Banks Swap Latin Debt." *New York Times,* September 11, 1986.

Falk, Pamela S. "Help Latins Trade Away Debt." *New York Times,* August 15, 1985.

————. "Mexico's Accession to the General Agreement on Tariffs and Trade (GATT)," unpublished case study of the Pew Initiative in Diplomatic Training; Columbia University, 1986.

Foxley, Alejandro. "The External Debt Problem from a Latin American Viewpoint," Working Paper no. 72. Notre Dame, Ind.: University of Notre Dame, Kellogg Institute, July 1986.

Guerrero, Israel Gutierrez; Kuenzler, Luis Tellex; and Wilcox, David. "Stop Mexico's Inflation and Eliminate the Deficit." *New York Times,* July 8, 1986.

Inter-American Development Bank. "Economic and Social Progress in Latin America: 1986 Report." Washington, D.C.: IDB, 1986.

Kim, Kwan S. "Mexico: The Debt Crisis and Options for Development Strategy," Working Paper no. 82. Notre Dame, Ind.: University of Notre Dame, Kellogg Institute, September 1986.

Latin American Monitor Ltd. "Mexico 1986." London, England: Latin American Monitor Ltd., 1986.

Morgan Guaranty Trust Company. "Growth and Financial Market Reform in Latin America." *World Financial Markets* (New York), April/May 1986.

Organization of American States. *Trade News,* vol. 2, no. 4, 1986.

Paz, Octavio. "Mexico and the United States: Positions and Counterpositions." in Tommie Sue Montgomery, ed., *Mexico Today.* Philadelphia, Pa.: Institute for the Study of Human Issues/Center for Inter-American Relations, 1982.

Rhodes, William R. "Remarks on Latin American Debt." Presentation to the Brazilian American Chamber of Commerce, June 11, 1986.

Riding, Alan. *Distant Neighbors: A Portrait of the Mexicans.* New York: Alfred Knopf, 1984.

Smith, Peter H. *Mexico: Neighbor in Transition,* Headline Series. New York: Foreign Policy Association, 1984.

Stepan, Alfred C. "Mexico Deserves Full U.S. Attention." *New York Times,* June 17, 1986.

Stockton, William. "Mexico Is Buying Back Some Debt at a Discount." *New York Times,* June 9, 1986.

————. "Mexican Pessimism Is Found in Survey." *New York Times,* November 16, 1986.

U.S. Congress, Joint Economic Committee. "The Impact of the Latin American Debt Crisis on the U.S. Economy." Washington, D.C.: U.S. Congress, May 10, 1986.

U.S. Department of Commerce. "Foreign Economic Trends and Their Implications for the United States." Washington, D.C.: U.S. Department of Commerce, International Trade Administration, April 1986.

U.S. International Trade Commission. "Operation of the Trade Agreements Program," 37th report, USITC Publication no. 1871. Washington, D.C.: Government Printing Office, June 1986.

PART ONE

The Political Economy of Oil: Mexico's Debt in the 1980s

1

Mexico: Is There Life After Debt?

Alan J. Stoga

In the 1970s the rapid increase in oil revenues and the growth of foreign debt fueled an economic boom in Mexico; in the 1980s excessive dependence on oil and the burden of an excessively large and expensive foreign debt have contributed to economic decline and despair. Since 1982 Mexico—the world's largest debtor and one of the largest oil exporters—has been trying to cope first with a debt crisis and then with an oil crisis. There has been a succession of oil policies, economic adjustment programs, debt delays, and restructurings, but the country has fundamentally failed to resolve either crisis; from some perspectives it has not even made any very impressive efforts.

Admittedly, the "solution" probably lies beyond the actions of any one country. The oil crisis (which, of course, has been a boom to oil consumers) reflects the imbalance between supply and demand, as well as the inability of producers to manage a cartel during a period of excess supply. The debt crisis reflects in part an underlying shift in economic relations between industrial and developing countries and, in part, a dramatic change in how industrial countries manage their own economies. Debtor countries have simply had to cope with the results.

Unfortunately, it would be hard to argue that Mexico has coped well. Despite massive new external borrowings, severe austerity, and several years of IMF-sanctioned stabilization programs, the economy shows no signs of returning to a path of sustainable economic growth or of lessened dependence on oil. Instead, the economy is stagnating, punctuated by short periods of economic expansion (e.g., from mid-1984 through mid-1985) and sharp contraction (e.g., 1986). Fluctuations in economic policy and oil prices explain most of the variation around the central tendency toward stagnation. Even following completion of the most recent financial and economic stabilization package in the last months of 1986, there is little reason for this pattern to change.

The Years 1983 and 1984: A False Dawn

Four years ago, Mexico announced that it would be unable to meet maturing principal and interest payments on its massive foreign debt. For the rest of Latin America—and indeed for much of the developing world—Mexico's debt problems triggered the international debt crisis that continues today. For Mexico the immediate consequences were a dramatic decline in real economic activity, an unprecedented increase in unemployment, and an inflationary explosion. The country, which had been considered a prime borrower by most international financial institutions during the late 1970s, was suddenly shut off from new credit.

In 1983 and 1984, Mexico was widely praised as the symbol of successful adjustment to the debt crisis. Under the leadership of President Miguel de la Madrid Hurtado and Finance Minister Jesus Silva Herzog, and with the strong support of the International Monetary Fund (IMF) and the U.S. government, the Mexicans designed and began to implement an economic stabilization program. They rescheduled external debt and, at least until the end of 1984, more or less lived within the economic and financial targets that had been agreed to with the IMF—this at a time when every other Latin American debtor was incapable of meeting its program targets.

In 1984-1985 economic activity recovered sharply, growing at a 6 to 7 percent pace from the second half of 1984 through mid-1985. The balance of payments improved dramatically, and surpluses on trade and current account were recorded. Business confidence seemed to recover, and the optimistic predictions of U.S. bankers that Mexico would be the first country to emerge from the debt crisis—at least as measured by renewed access to voluntary lending (as opposed to the "forced" or "involuntary" lending associated with refinancing and rescheduling)—seemed to many to be on the verge of realization.

In 1986, the collapse of oil prices again plunged Mexico into financial and economic crisis. The economy contracted, inflation rose toward triple digits, and a multi-billion-dollar emergency loan package was drawn up. A new stabilization program was negotiated, and Mexico has once more had to renew its commitment to economic adjustment. Despite the earlier optimism, emergence from the debt crisis now seems to be a distant goal at best—a change attributable, in the conventional wisdom, largely to the chaos in international oil markets.

Unfortunately, the conventional wisdom is a misreading of economic statistics and a misinterpretation of what has occurred in Mexico over the past several years: Even though the sharp drop in oil revenues precipitated a renewed crisis, the lack of thorough economic reform made it inevitable. The corrections that had been achieved were largely

TABLE 1.1
Mexico: Growth and Inflation (% change)

	1981	1982	1983	1984	1985	1986
Real GDP	8.0	-0.5	-5.3	3.7	2.7	-4 to -6
Consumer prices	27.9	59.0	101.8	65.5	57.9	100

Source: Banco de Mexico, various publications; author's projections.

transitory and served mainly to meet short-term IMF and creditor bank obligations rather than to attain lasting structural changes. Public-sector finances were not fundamentally improved; investment incentives remained weak; exchange rate adjustment was periodically allowed to lag behind domestic inflation, thus discouraging capital repatriation and encouraging new capital flight; monetary expansion was excessive; and inflation remained high. Despite rescheduling and the accumulation of current account surpluses, external debt has continued to grow and debt service remains an almost unmanageable burden on the balance of payments, the government budget, and the economy.

The numbers are mind numbing: During four years of "adjustment," total foreign debt has risen by some $11 billion, the economy contracted by at least 3 percent, and the inflation rate has averaged more than 70 percent per year (see Table 1.1). Real standards of living have fallen dramatically as the purchasing power of wage earners has declined to levels reached in the 1960s and as unemployment has risen. Migration to the United States—as an escape valve for Mexicans seeking greater economic and political security—has apparently grown exponentially; in similar fashion, the flight of Mexican capital has continued, totaling as much as $17 billion since the end of 1982 (and many times more in the preceding years), according to an estimate published in March 1986 by Morgan Guaranty in *World Financial Markets.*

Perhaps even more disturbing than this litany of economic failures is the continuing uncertainty about the future. The collapse of oil prices in 1986 demonstrated the extent to which the country's prospects remain dependent on oil. The erratic implementation of stabilization programs over the past four years produced more austerity than economic reform and failed to loosen the ties to oil or to lay the groundwork for renewed growth. Inevitably, failure has eroded at least some of the political basis for renewed stabilization efforts.

The resulting dilemma is that in the absence of economic reform, resumption of sustained economic growth is not possible; and without economic growth, the political will to support reform may be impossible to muster. Moreover, such growth has to be financed in the short run through enlarged export earnings (i.e., primarily through increased oil exports), increased foreign borrowings, or capital flight repatriation. The first of these options seems unlikely, and the second one is undesirable, although the current IMF–World Bank–commercial bank program is predicated on the assumption that more debt is inevitable. Finally, sustained repatriation of flight capital will occur only in a stable economic and political environment that offers attractive investment opportunities—but this, too, is unlikely to be the case in 1987-1988.

The real failure of the past four years, then, is that Mexico has not been able to break out of the vicious circle of increased borrowing to finance growth and continued interest payments. Assessing blame—to the Mexican government that failed to reform the economy; to the international creditors who failed to design more flexible, long-term, and realistic refinancing programs; to the U.S. government, which failed to recognize (or, if it recognized, to act on) the overwhelming importance to U.S. national security of achieving economic reform and sustainable growth in Mexico; to the oil producers who failed to design a strategy that might have cushioned the fall of oil prices—does not change these facts.

The Mexican government and political elites may now be prepared to make a sustained effort at reforming the economy. Indeed, the current stabilization program is supposed to produce a fundamental reform of the trading system, the privatization of at least some major public-sector industrial companies, and increased foreign investments as well as renewed economic growth. However, fiscal policy remains far too lax, shifting too much of the adjustment burden to the monetary and exchange rate side and forcing the private sector once again to bear a disproportionate share of the costs of stabilization. Although the current program represents a significant step forward—at least as compared to its predecessors—it does not go far enough in redressing the economy's ills.

Unfortunately, the likely result is that the country's recovery from the economic and financial collapse of 1982-1983 will continue to be slow and uneven. In 1986, the economy contracted by at least 4 percent and perhaps as much as 6 percent. In 1987 the government hopes for a rebound of perhaps 3.5 percent, but at best it will be years before the dynamism of the late 1970s is recaptured, or even before the economy again grows fast enough to make a dent in the now massive unemployment. The cost in political terms could be high: The government, the dominant political party (the Institutionalized Revolutionary party, or PRI), and public institutions already lack credibility and seem to be losing legitimacy. These factors are likely to strain the country's ability to sustain

TABLE 1.2
Mexico: Balance of Payments ($ billions)

	1981	1982	1983	1984	1985	1986
Exports	20.9	22.1	23.1	25.4	23.1	15.5
Oil	14.6	16.5	16.0	16.6	14.8	5.6
Imports	24.0	14.4	8.6	11.3	13.5	12.0
Trade balance	-3.1	7.6	14.6	14.1	9.6	3.5
Current account balance	-12.7	-6.4	5.1	4.0	0.5	-3.5

Source: Banco de Mexico, various publications; projections by Mexican authorities, July 1986.

the kind of structural economic changes that are essential to eventual lasting recovery.

Economic Adjustment

Despite the criticisms, there have been several important accomplishments of the economic adjustment efforts that began in the fall of 1982. The current account of the balance of payments has shifted from a cumulative deficit of $30 billion in 1979–1982 to a total surplus of around $10 billion in 1983–1985 (see Table 1.2). This was accomplished not only through a sharp reduction of imports (even after an almost 70 percent increase in 1984-1985, imports in 1985 were only slightly more than one-half the 1981 level) but also through increases in exports, especially nonpetroleum exports. Sales of such goods rose by $2 billion between 1981 and 1985, an increase of more than one-third. Many private-sector companies, under intense financial pressures, began to export for the first time during these years.

Over the past four years, foreign reserves rose from less than $1 billion to more than $5 billion at the end of 1985, although they reportedly declined by at least $1 billion during the first half of 1986. During the same years, private companies actually reduced their foreign indebtedness (the growth in public debt was more than accounted for by the rise in total foreign debt). Contributing to these financial improvements has been the current account surplus and at least some reduction in capital flight. Capital flight, which totaled at least $20 billion in 1981-1982 (and reached an estimated $16 billion in 1976–1980) apparently slowed in 1983–1985. (Estimates of capital flight, by their very nature, are difficult to substantiate. The aforementioned $17 billion figure for 1983–1985, for instance, is viewed by many as being too high.) Moreover, during the first five months of 1986, capital flight was reversed as Mexican entrepreneurs apparently repatriated capital to offset tight domestic credit conditions.

Domestically, a sharp reduction in the public sector deficit occurred prior to 1986. As a share of gross domestic product (GDP), the deficit, which had been almost 19 percent in 1982, was reduced to around 8 percent in 1983 and 1984 and to 10 percent in 1985. Though too high for monetary stabilization and considerably higher than IMF target levels, this performance represented a significant improvement. In 1986, however, the loss of oil-related revenues and, even more important, the continuing rise in interest payments on public debt produced a sharp rise in the deficit that the government estimates to have reached 17 percent of GDP.

The 1983–1985 improvement in the public deficit in part reflects an important reduction in government spending on goods and nonfinancial services. Such spending declined by 5 percentage points of GDP; more than half of this reduction came from capital expenditures. In an economy where the public sector directly accounts for 22 percent of domestic value added, such a reduction in government-controlled investment spending has a powerful contractionary effect on the economy.

Indeed, the large (and growing) public-sector deficit reflects to a considerable degree the cost of financing the rising public-sector debt burden. The Mexican government argues that its so-called primary deficit (the total deficit minus interest payments) has shifted from a deficit equal to 9.4 percent of GDP in 1981 (compared with a total deficit, including interest payments, of 14.4 percent) to a *surplus* of 3.3 percent in 1985 and a projected surplus of 3.2 percent in 1986. In other words, interest payments have increased "uncontrollably" with rising debt and rising real interest rates, whereas the controllable portion of the deficit has been eliminated. (Note that the same argument would dramatically improve perceptions of the U.S. budget situation as well; note, furthermore, that it is the overall financial deficit which burdens an economy, by absorbing the bulk of available credit and forcing interest rates higher.)

The most impressive accomplishments of the past four years, including the rescheduling of massive amounts of public and private foreign debt, have been made in the balance of payments rather than in the internal economy. The de la Madrid administration pursued sharply contractionary policies in 1982-1983 (thus contributing to a reduction of imports), dramatically devalued the exchange rate and converted negative real domestic interest rates to positive ones (thus encouraging exports and making capital flight more costly), and benefited from a strong U.S. economic recovery. Balance of payments adjustment was forced on the government largely by external factors—the collapse of the exchange rate as a result of the massive exodus of flight capital in 1981-1982 and the sudden disappearance of foreign credit—and its immediate response was to an economic crisis defined initially in those terms.

Of course, some of the Mexican authorities and their international overseers recognized the domestic roots of the country's crisis. The economy of the 1970s was characterized by corruption, misallocation of resources, heavy-handed government regulation, lack of market incentives, rapid government spending growth, excessive monetary creation, unrealistic exchange rates, and other ill-advised economic policies. Yet the economy grew, if anything, too quickly following the start of the oil boom in the mid-1970s. The economy became overheated, inflation accelerated, foreign borrowing ballooned (indeed, foreign debt doubled from 1979 to 1982, reaching $91 billion), and a crisis became inevitable.

Unfortunately, the adjustment efforts of 1983–1985 only half-heartedly addressed these problems. Inflation remains high: Consumer prices, which increased more than 100 percent in 1983, rose 65 percent in 1984 and 58 percent in 1985, and increased at a much faster rate in 1986. In 1985, the controlled exchange rate was allowed to lag well behind relative price increases, and external competitiveness was eroded. A series of exchange market reforms in July 1985 amounted to a de facto, but partial, devaluation. Even after the reforms, a 33 percent gap hovered between the controlled rate and the much lower free-market rate. At the end of 1985, the market rate was 448 pesos per dollar; by the end of July it had depreciated to 642 pesos per dollar, more than a 40 percent change. In 1986 the exchange rate remained relatively stable in the early months of the year—buoyed by inflows of Mexican private capital—but came under enormous pressure as the decline in oil prices intensified.

Although real wages have fallen since the onset of the crisis—as much as 40 percent by some calculations—public-sector wage policy has helped to sustain the inflationary momentum. Although inflation had begun to decline, the government granted minimum wage increases of 30 percent in January and 20 percent in June 1984. Given the depressed labor markets—that is, rising unemployment and falling employment—no gain in real wages was expected; the sharp rate rises helped to reignite inflationary expectations. Indeed, in 1984 and 1985 wages roughly kept pace with inflation.

Monetary policy, however, has been the driving force behind the recent inflationary experience in Mexico. The money supply (M2) grew 54 percent in 1982, 41 percent in 1983, and 62 percent in 1984. In 1985 money growth accelerated throughout the first three quarters of the year; by September the money supply was almost 70 percent above the preceding year's level. Unfortunately, this acceleration came at a

time when inflation had been slowing, thus once again renewing inflationary expectations. The Bank of Mexico responded to this situation
by sharply tightening credit throughout the fourth quarter and the first
months of 1986. This policy raised interest rates and almost completely
dried up the availability of credit to the private sector.

The need to tighten credit dramatically in part reflected the slow
progress that has been made in improving public finances. Indeed, the
most important part of the reduction in the public-sector deficit came
from increased taxes and public tariffs rather than from spending cuts.
High marginal tax rates were further increased; the federal sales tax
was raised and the prices of historically highly subsidized public utilities
(including gasoline) adjusted sharply upward. The overall size of government, both in relation to the total economy and in terms of its
impact on the private sector, has not significantly declined.

The cost of these policies is measured in the eroding value of the
Mexican peso, periodic renewed waves of capital flight, weak investment
activity and—given the slowdown in export growth because of U.S.
economic weakness and falling oil prices—renewed recession. Most
important, public and private investment bore a disproportionate share
of the 1982-1983 economic decline. During this period, real GDP fell
by almost 6 percent (per capita GDP dropped twice as fast), but
investment declined 45 percent in real terms. Coupled with capital flight
and a sharp drop in foreign investment inflows, this decline in investment
meant that the economy's productive capacity—which, in any event,
was of doubtful value in some sectors—declined sharply.

The economic strategy adopted in 1982 and more or less continued
into 1986 essentially had two objectives. First, there was to be a quick
adjustment of the balance of payments to the twin realities of limited
availability of new credit (following the orgy of borrowing in 1980–1982)
and declining oil prices. There was also to be a quick deflation to bring
Mexico's standard of living into line with its dramatically reduced
earnings capability and prospects and to arrest consumer price rises.

The second objective of the strategy was a gradual adjustment of
underlying economic structures to reduce dependence on foreign savings
and foreign goods. This was to be accomplished in large part through
the creation of domestic savings and investment incentives, the maintenance of a competitive (or even overly competitive) exchange rate,
reduced subsidies, monetary policies that ratified the changes in relative
prices, and a reduction in the size of the public sector.

The first phase of the strategy was obviously implemented. The
balance of payments shift was greater than expected, and the standard
of living contracted, though not in a way or to a degree sufficient to
undermine the inflationary momentum in the economy. But progress

on structural adjustment has been slow, and the country may be tiring of adjustment without the real prospect of sustained adequate growth.

The concept of "adequate" growth, defined relative to the growth rate of the population and the labor force, is an important one to understand. Mexico's population of 75 million is expected to grow 2.4 percent annually through the decade, and the government anticipates that the total will exceed 88 million by 1990. Moreover, the very high birth rates of the 1950s and 1960s have led to an acceleration in the growth of the labor force, which is expected to increase 3.5 percent annually through 1990. In practical terms, 750,000 to 1 million new jobs per year would have to be created each year to meet these population demands.

Historical patterns suggest that in the absence of substantial emigration, the economy would have to grow at least 5 percent annually to prevent unemployment from increasing. Even optimistic medium-term forecasts do not anticipate such rapid growth. One obvious conclusion to be drawn, then, is that emigration, mostly to the United States, will continue and probably accelerate.

In any event, per capita economic activity has declined and unemployment and underemployment have risen since the onset of the economic crisis in 1982. Moreover, the severe socioeconomic consequences of this crisis have been only partly offset by the subsidies on food and other basics that have been maintained at least to some extent.

It is important to remember that Mexico has one of the world's most unequal distributions of income: The top one-fifth of the population receives over half of the national income, while the bottom half receives less than 15 percent. This distribution has almost certainly worsened in the past four years; although all segments of the population have been badly affected by the recession, those at the lower end of the income scale are particularly worse off. Moreover, although Mexico's population is not necessarily a constraint on growth, its large size and rapid growth mean that if the economy continues to stagnate, the economic pie will have to be cut into smaller and smaller pieces.

Economic Constraints

Without a renewed commitment to the kinds of thoroughgoing economic (and perhaps political) reforms that the Mexican authorities have thus far avoided, Mexico will be condemned either to a kind of stagflation—which could have severe political consequences because of the distribution effects—or to a stop-go pattern of alternating economic growth and decline. The latter prospect could be equally difficult po-

TABLE 1.3
Mexico: Debt and Debt Service ($ billions and %)

	1981	1982	1983	1984	1985	1986(p)
Total foreign debt	77.3	91.2	93.8	96.6	98.0	103.0
Interest payments	8.4	12.2	10.2	11.7	9.9	8.6
Interest as % of exports	27.7	44.4	35.9	36.4	33.7	55.5

Source: Banco de Mexico, various publications; author's estimates and projections.

litically in that it might frustrate the expectations of Mexico's young and rapidly growing labor force.

Before considering the current stabilization effort and the prospects for the next two years, we will find it useful to look at the constraints likely to limit the country's economic potential for some time to come.

First, of course, is the need to service the foreign debt, which totaled $98 billion at the end of 1985 and was expected by the Mexican authorities to total around $103 billion by the end of 1986—if all of the new borrowing requests are satisfied (Table 1.3). As Mexico has succeeded in rescheduling $48.7 billion in commercial bank debt over the next fourteen years (and, more important, as the country has no prospect of actually repaying debt in the sense of reducing its gross debt burden under any foreseeable circumstance), the interest burden is more significant than the total. Interest payments were estimated to be around $9 billion last year—that is, about 50 percent of export earnings. Lower interest rates and faster export growth would reduce this figure (each one percentage point change in interest rates changes the gross interest bill by almost $1 billion), but the reduction in interest rates that has occurred over the past two years unfortunately reflected slower U.S. growth, which in turn contributed to lower export earnings (because of weaker demand for both oil and nonoil exports). Most long-run forecasts indicate that interest payments are likely to equal at least one-third of hard currency earnings by 1990, even with sustained export growth.

Second, there is the decapitalization of the economy. Capital flight during 1976–1985 has been estimated at $53 billion; during the same years the increase in foreign debt was $75 billion. These capital outflows not only inflated the foreign debt numbers but also undercut productive investment.

Third, the legacy of economic mismanagement and the shock of the 1982 collapse had a disproportionate effect on the private sector. Private companies, including joint ventures with foreign investors, have been burdened by the massive devaluation, the curtailing of access to foreign credit, the limits on availability of domestic credit, the contraction of domestic demand, the limited availability of imported inputs, and the uncertainty of a generally difficult business environment. In 1984 some companies began to revive, but the tightening of economic policy in the second half of 1985 and in 1986 as oil prices fell curtailed their recovery, with the possible exception of those companies that have carved out export businesses.

Fourth, weak prospects for both oil price and demand directly affect export as well as budgetary revenues and indirectly affect the overall pace of economic activity. Some two-thirds of export revenues and one-third of government revenues have come from the hydrocarbon sector in recent years. By contrast, in 1986 oil exports are likely to account for only one-third of total exports. This latter statistic reflects not only the precipitous decline in oil prices (in July 1986 Mexico's average export price was $8.26, less than one-third the level at the end of 1985) but also the problems involved in marketing the country's production. Thus, although the publicly stated policy was to export as much as 1.5 million barrels per day (bpd), actual exports in the first six months of the year were under 1.2 million bpd and were disastrously lower at times during the first quarter. (In August, Mexico announced it would limit output to 1.35 million bpd in an effort to cooperate with an OPEC production agreement.) Similar shortfalls have occurred in the past, reflecting misguided efforts to support OPEC as well as simple marketing mistakes. However, even perfect marketing techniques cannot offset extremely weak prices; the government is now assuming that oil revenues will be only $6 billion in 1987, with an average price of $11 per barrel and export volumes of 1.3 million bpd. In contrast, oil exports earned $16.5 billion in 1982, when the debt crisis began.

Fifth, Mexican authorities have decided to force industry to become more competitive by reducing domestic protection, substituting tariffs for quantitive restrictions (including import licenses), and committing to a program of phased tariff reductions. Much of the industry that developed in the 1960s and 1970s behind high tariff and nontariff barriers is inefficient and internationally uncompetitive. If the economy is opened to greater competition (assuming the balance of payments can support more imports), domestic industry will come under renewed pressure. In the short run this adjustment will weaken the economy, but it is essential for the long run.

Sixth, protectionist restrictions on nonoil Mexican exports to the United States could seriously hinder the country's export-led recovery. Manufactured goods, although starting from a small base, have grown rapidly and hold considerable promise for the future. The list of complaints filed against Mexican products in the United States during the past year or two is a long one, and more cases seem to be forthcoming. However, Mexico's recent accession to the General Agreement on Trade and Tariffs (GATT), as well as a recent agreement whereby Mexico dropped certain subsidies in return for more favorable treatment under U.S. trade laws, may help to offset the general increase of protectionist sentiment in the United States.

Last, the course of the U.S. economy will have significant consequences for Mexico. The current emphasis on increasing exports, most of which are going to the United States, will have the unwelcome result of binding the U.S. and Mexican economies more closely together. While this economic binding has important political implications, it also means that Mexican growth will be increasingly sensitive to fluctuations in U.S. economic conditions.

Most of these constraints were foreseeable four years ago when Mexico was forced by the onset of the economic crisis to undertake its stabilization program. At that time the country's greatest hope for long-term recovery was clearly to implement as thorough an adjustment program as possible, utilizing the good will that newly elected President de la Madrid brought to office to weather the inevitable economic decline. With the U.S. economy rapidly expanding and Mexico's oil revenues more or less steady, the country could have used the 1983-1984 period to make necessary structural changes. Instead, the government (and its foreign creditors) focused mainly on the symptoms of the economic problem— the balance of payments and the structure of foreign debt.

The New Stabilization Program

In 1986 yet another stabilization program was constructed as a response to both the oil price collapse and the cumulative failure of the past several years. The new program seeks to cushion the Mexican economy's adjustment to the drop in oil revenues through substantial new compensatory borrowing from commercial banks and international financial institutions, totaling some $12 billion during 1986-1987. It has also established two new and important principles: first, that further shortfalls in oil revenues would elicit additional lending, more or less automatically, and, second, that slower than projected growth (3.5 percent in 1987) would produce more lending as well. In addition, it reduced the spread it pays on existing loans from commercial banks.

Although the details are still somewhat unclear, foreign debt by the end of 1987 is expected to total around $108 billion, with foreign reserves of $7 to $8 billion. By comparison, total debt at the end of 1985 was $98 billion and reserves were just over $5 billion.

In terms of economic policy there are several important elements of the program:

- Mexico will maintain positive real interest rates and a realistic exchange rate.
- The public-sector deficit is to be reduced (at least from what it would have been) through tax increases and improved collections, subsidy reductions, and spending cuts totaling the equivalent of three percentage points of GDP by the end of 1987. However, the overall financial deficit is forecast by the Mexican authorities to be around 17 percent of GDP in 1986 and only marginally less in 1987.
- The system of subsidies is to be further revised, including fee increases and new delivery mechanisms that focus subsidies on the lower income classes rather than extending them to the general population.
- Foreign investment will be more aggressively encouraged—but on a case-by-case basis rather than through a change in the restrictive legislation that governs such investments.
- Privatization is to be pursued outside of strategic industries, and noneconomic state enterprises are to be modernized, restructured, or closed.
- The shift to a trading system based on tariffs instead of quantitative restrictions (e.g., import licenses) is to be completed, tariffs are to be gradually reduced, and the official pricing system (under which the government sets the import prices that form the basis for duties) is to be eliminated by the end of 1987. Considerable progress has already been made in this area, including membership in GATT, a reduction of the share of imports subject to quantitative restrictions from 80 percent in 1982 to 45 percent in 1986, and a significant reduction of average tariff barriers.
- Dollar indexed deposit accounts are being introduced to discourage capital flight.

In terms of the timing and pace of Mexico's recovery, this program relies too heavily on new market-priced foreign borrowing, which adds to the economically (and politically) unsustainable debt burden; in addition, the program makes only modest efforts, given the dimensions of the problem, toward reducing the budget deficit. The deterioration in the 1986 budget is more attributable to the rise in interest costs (totaling the equivalent of about 6 percent of GDP), mostly on domestic debt, than to the decline in budget revenues derived from the oil sector (projected to be equal to about 3 percent of GDP); budgeted spending cuts reduce the rise in the 1986 deficit to some 7 percent of GDP. These shortcomings are somewhat understandable in a political context: At this point in the political cycle, Mexican officials must carefully balance the economy's needs for stabilization with their estimates of what costs are politically bearable. Unfortunately, the former is rising, whereas the latter is probably falling.

Nevertheless, the promised further reforms of the trading system and the rationalization of the public sector are important and, potentially, long-lasting structural changes. Already surfacing in 1986 were two symbolically significant developments indicating that the Mexican government will show more constancy in its current efforts. First, the entry into GATT ended a long, hotly contested debate over the appropriate trade policy for Mexico. The country will now have the opportunity to participate in the new multilateral trade round, but, more important, its producers will have an even greater incentive to improve their efficiency and competitiveness. Second, the government announced the closing of an obsolete steel company, Fundidora de Monterrey, which resulted in the laying off of more than 6,000 public workers and signaled that the government seriously intends to shrink the size of the public sector.

Despite all these changes, however, Mexico remains an oil economy. In the summer of 1986, Mexican oil prices were less than $10 per barrel. Every $1 decline in price changes export revenues by $550 million at full export production; every $1 roughly equals 2 percent of government revenue. The decline in revenues during 1986 has been estimated by the U.S. government as equal to 25 percent of government revenue and 5–6 percent of GDP. If prices fall further, imports (and economic activity) will be curtailed—even if the decline is partially compensated by increased borrowing. And too much borrowing would create a more or less permanent overhang that, in turn, would cripple economic potential.

Unfortunately, both the balance of payments and the budgetary effects of lower revenues have tended to be exaggerated by the government's habit of reacting slowly to changing economic conditions and by the Mexican public's skepticism about government policy, as evidenced by capital flight. The most persistent example of the former pertains to exchange rate policy, which has repeatedly contributed to the economic crisis. For example, Mexican officials once again allowed the peso to become overvalued in 1985, thereby hurting export growth, contributing to capital flight, and setting the stage for the 1986 peso crisis.

The oil constraint, the need for further economic reforms, and the weakness of the U.S. economy probably mean that the Mexican economy will be hard-pressed to grow faster than 2–3 percent through the end of this year and into 1988. But this increased growth will barely compensate for the sharp drop in economic activity in 1986; indeed, the economic growth rate over the whole three years, 1986–1988, will possibly be as low as zero. As a result, the economy will be unable to generate enough new jobs to meet the demand of the rapidly growing labor force, and the standard of living for most Mexicans will continue to stagnate or decline.

The Mexican government's IMF-sanctioned stabilization program anticipates 3.5 percent growth in 1987, and creditors have committed to making additional funding available if the growth rate is lower. Indeed, such loans are likely to be quite necessary, given that most engines of growth—exports, investment, and consumer demand—will probably remain weak. Whether additional imports of raw materials, spare parts, and the like (which the incremental loans are intended to finance) will be adequate to spur growth is unclear. At present, in fact, the economy seems to suffer not so much from a shortage of financing as from other ailments.

At the same time, inflation will slow only gradually given the combination of loose fiscal policy—the large deficit—and relatively tight monetary policy. (By contrast, these two conditions worked to reduce U.S. inflation dramatically. However, the United States enjoyed the luxury of massive capital inflows to ease the financing constraint, the benefits of a rising currency to reduce import costs, and, more recently, sharp drops in the price of imported commodities. Mexico is obviously in very different circumstances.) Undoubtedly, the pattern of 1982–1984 will be repeated, with inflation in 1987 dropping to the 50–70 percent range at best.

The combined growth and inflation outlook will do little either to ease the pressure on the private sector (again, with the exception of the companies that have learned to export and have secured overseas markets) or to reduce unemployment and underemployment.

Admittedly, four years after the onset of Mexico's debt crisis, this forecast makes grim reading. If "life after debt" is so unpleasant and fraught with dangers for the one country in the Western Hemisphere that at least made an effort not only to play by the rules of the IMF and the creditor banks but also to undertake sustained economic reform, what are the implications for the others?

Although this formulation may exaggerate the coherence and constancy of the Mexican economic program—indeed, the Mexicans should have paid more attention to inflation, to reducing the size and powers of the public sector, and to the needs of the private sector—it nevertheless suggests that other highly indebted countries face even more uncertain prospects. Although many of these other countries have also succeeded in improving their balance of payments positions (like Mexico, largely by curtailing imports and by taking advantage of the unparalleled and unexpected U.S. import boom), they have failed to make much headway in recreating the conditions for sustained economic growth.

This scenario could translate into a new phase of the hemisphere-wide debt crisis. Slower export growth, reduced access even to official credits (because of failure to sustain stabilization efforts), renewed capital flight, and further private-sector investment weakness would undermine even the limited degree of economic recovery evidenced in 1984-1985. Badly battered by the 1982-1983 economic declines and the very uneven character of economic performance in the past eighteen months, the people of various Latin countries might be less willing to suffer renewed "austerity." Governments that have pursued adjustment programs either too halfheartedly (as in the Mexican case) or too incompetently may find it difficult to sustain their own legitimacy, to say nothing of their ability to establish a renewed program of economic reform.

Yet this admittedly worst-case scenario could be avoided by a new burst of strong U.S. economic growth or inspired and creative political leadership in the United States as well as in the major debtor countries, including Mexico. Unfortunately, neither prospect seems very likely. The Baker Initiative announced by U.S. Treasury Secretary James Baker in October 1985 has proven to have little substance, although some commentators and U.S. government officials describe the 1986 Mexican stabilization program as evidence of the Baker Initiative at work. However, the Baker Initiative was supposed to combine significant economic policy reform with adequate financing; the Mexican package is long on financing and short on reform.

Indeed, many other debtor countries—Argentina, Philippines, Nigeria, and others—seem to see the most recent Mexican package as a model for themselves. Such factors as (1) contingent lending facilities linked to commodity export revenues or to growth performance rather than to economic policies, (2) an emphasis on gradual changes in economic structures rather than orthodox fiscal policy discipline, (3) long-term debt rescheduling, and (4) large-scale availability of new financial resources are attractive to political leaders who have been presiding over stagnant economies. Such packages are seen as forcing at least part of the burden of adjustment onto creditors (and, perhaps, as delaying the politically difficult but inevitable budget cutting and economic reform for successors). Unfortunately, this is an unlikely formula for economic or, ultimately, political stability.

For its part, the United States should recognize that Mexican stability is an essential *U.S.* national security issue. Low, uneven, badly distributed growth (if there is any growth at all) is an unlikely formula for political calm. Such performance would accelerate Mexican emigration to the United States, encourage the breakdown of Mexican political institutions, foster a jingoistic anti-Americanism among Mexican politicians, and increase tensions between the two governments.

In fairness, Washington may understand these risks and the urgency of helping Mexico to help itself. The Federal Reserve and the U.S. Treasury were prime movers in constructing the 1986 economic stabilization program and its predecessors. And within the context of the debt strategy articulated by Secretary Baker, the U.S. government has been relatively forthcoming.

Unfortunately, however, this approach may not be adequate on either economic grounds (oil prices are too low, Mexico's accumulated debt is too large, and its economy is too badly in need of reform) or political grounds. The political point is not that Mexicans have already endured four years of weak economic activity in the name of "stabilization" or "adjustment," or even that the current Mexican government is entering the traditional "lame duck" phase during which a successor to President de la Madrid will be chosen, thus making the implementation of politically sensitive economic reforms even more perilous.

Rather, the point is that the United States has thus far failed to establish a bilateral political framework in which the whole range of sensitive issues—trade, debt, growth, migration, investment, drugs, and so on—can be addressed as part of an integrated whole. Together, these pieces amount to what may be one of the most important national security issues facing the United States in the closing years of the twentieth century. Removed from the multilateral context, these pieces could provide opportunities for skillful and farsighted politicians to design a new bilateral relationship. The goal of such a relationship would be to maximize economic growth and opportunity in both countries. The means would be to understand the linkages among various economic and political issues and to trade concessions in one area (e.g., on Mexican debt held by U.S. banks) for reciprocal concessions in another (e.g., trade or investment advantages for U.S. companies).

Such an approach would not obviate the need for economic reform. But it might provide an environment conducive to a more generous infusion of resources (if it comes down to this, is Egypt or Mexico more central to U.S. national security?) and a more positive political momentum than that which emanates from avoiding default or sustaining interest payments.

Otherwise, "life after debt" for Mexico will continue to be politically and economically dangerous—a prospect that, in turn, would inevitably affect the key interests of the United States. For Mexico's creditors, who spent too much of the past several years basking in self-congratulation over having successfully managed the debt crisis, the result could be even worse.

2

The Impact of the Debt Crisis on the Mexican Political System

Susan Kaufman Purcell

Political Stability

The onset of Mexico's economic crisis in August 1982 produced a profound sense of pessimism, both within Mexico and abroad, regarding the prospects for continued political stability in the country. The reasons for this pessimism seemed obvious. For nearly forty years, Mexico's economy had experienced continuous and often spectacular levels of economic growth. Few observers doubted that there was an important and positive correlation between the continually expanding economy and the political stability that had made Mexico unique in comparison with its Latin American neighbors. It therefore seemed to follow that Mexico's economic crisis, which would usher in a period of low or no economic growth, would probably prove harmful to the Mexican political system and perhaps ultimately undermine it.

As of 1986, more than four years have passed since the onset of the crisis. The unmitigated pessimism that took hold in 1982 has been replaced by a generally cautious optimism regarding Mexico's economic and political prospects. What accounts for the better-than-expected outcome of the past few years? There are several factors, but chief among them has been Mexico's ability to implement an austerity program that has more or less met the goals mutually agreed upon by Mexico and the International Monetary Fund. The costs have been high: Imports were cut drastically, producing two years of negative economic growth; per capita income declined; and unemployment, combined with under-employment, reached an estimated 40–50 percent.

Despite such economic hardship, the political system has held firm. People did not take to the streets as was originally feared, nor did the labor movement engage in work stoppages or widespread strikes. The political leaders pulled together rather than apart, and the military's influence in the political system did not significantly increase, as many had originally predicted would happen.

Much of the credit goes to President de la Madrid and his astute handling of the crisis. The economic team he chose was widely reputed to be the best in Latin America, and the high respect in which it was held in the international financial community served Mexico well throughout the difficult and sensitive debt negotiations. In the political sphere, President de la Madrid proved to be an effective leader despite his essentially technocratic background. He was helped, of course, by the Mexican people, who were willing to follow his lead and endure great sacrifices. He was also helped by a political system that proved to be considerably more institutionalized, flexible, and resilient than even the most informed observers of Mexico had believed it to be.

Unemployment

The most pressing problem is perhaps unemployment and the negative political repercussions it could have. Even before August 1982, Mexico was faced with a severe unemployment problem. Although the rate of population increase has slowed to an estimated 2.7 percent annually (from a high of approximately 3.5 percent several years ago), more than 800,000 new jobs must still be created each year in order to keep pace with the growth of the labor force. Mexico reached this target only once, in 1980, by accelerating economic growth to 8 percent. The undesirable side effects, however, included a substantial increase in the inflation rate, excessive government spending, and an overvaluation of the peso.

There is little prospect that Mexico will be able to solve its unemployment problem in the foreseeable future. As economic growth will be considerably slower than the rate that characterized the years of Mexico's so-called oil boom, Mexico will have to find other ways to provide jobs for new entrants to the labor force. These might include increased emphasis on labor-intensive investment as well as the creation of policies to increase productivity in the agricultural sector in particular. In the meantime, the fact that Mexico shares a largely unpoliced 2,000-mile border with the United States will continue to constitute a partial "solution" to Mexico's unemployment problem, even with the new immigration bill that purportedly increases U.S. control over its borders. Accordingly, the U.S.-Mexican border will probably remain fairly porous and continue to provide a kind of "safety" valve for Mexico's surplus labor into the foreseeable future.

The Government and the Labor Movement

Related to the issue of unemployment is the more general issue of relations between the Mexican government and the labor movement. Mexico's political stability has in great part depended on a cooperative and mutually beneficial relationship between government and labor. Labor leaders served two masters—the government and their rank and file. They contributed to the success of government policies by keeping labor demands under control. Their reward was considerable wealth and patronage, some of which the leaders used for their own ends and some of which was distributed to the rank and file in order to strengthen the control and authority of the labor leadership. Although union members have not prospered as much as they might have hoped under this arrangement, they did achieve a relatively privileged economic status in comparison to other groups in the population.

Several factors have been undermining the traditional relationship between government and labor in Mexico. The first is inflation. Until recently, Mexico was unaccustomed to high rates of inflation; when the inflation rate reached 30 percent during the administration of President López Portillo, it was regarded as extremely high. The traditionally low rate of inflation that Mexico enjoyed until the late 1970s had facilitated cooperation between the government and labor by providing an economic environment that did not provoke a continuing escalation of labor's demands on the government. By the end of 1982, however, at the height of the economic crisis, inflation had exceeded 100 percent. Although progress has been made in reducing inflation since then, it must be decreased further if Mexico is to avoid the cycle of escalating inflation and wage demands that have characterized other Latin American countries.

Another development that could destabilize traditional relations between the government and the labor movement would be the death of Fidel Velázquez, the leader of Mexico's main labor confederation, the Confederación de Trabajadores de México (CTM). Now in his eighties, Velazquez is usually credited with having played a major role in the establishment and continuation of the cooperative relationship between the government and labor. Whether the person chosen as his successor will be able to follow in his footsteps remains an unanswered question.

Another unanswered question involves the rise of so-called independent unions, which do not belong to the CTM or other large, geographically organized labor confederations. Rather, these independent unions are industry based, and their members and leaders are better educated than those of the large labor confederations. Traditional political methods of control and co-optation will probably prove less successful with these unions and their leaders. One of the challenges facing the Mexican political system in coming years, therefore, is the establishment of a cooperative and mutually beneficial working relationship between the Mexican government and the more sophisticated independent unions.

The Government and the Middle Class

The relationship between the government and the middle class has also been profoundly affected by the economic crisis. Mexico's middle class benefited greatly from the Mexican Revolution of 1910 and the economic and political systems established in its aftermath. Because many members of the middle class are salaried white-collar workers, however, they have been hit especially hard by the high rates of inflation. They have also suffered from the repeated devaluation of the peso, which has made it difficult for them to continue living in the style to which they were accustomed. This style included frequent travel abroad and the easy importation of luxury items.

Whether members of the middle class will express their discontent by parading through the streets of Mexico City banging pots and pans, as their counterparts in several South American countries have done, remains to be seen. So far, they have chosen less confrontational ways of demonstrating their unhappiness. On the economic side, they have transferred significant financial assets abroad, thereby contributing to the capital flight that is estimated to be at least $30 billion. Politically, they have protested by voting for the major opposition political party, the Partido de Acción Nacional (PAN). This is particularly true of the middle-class inhabitants of Mexico's northern cities, who tend to emulate the citizens of the United States and criticize and resist control by the central government in Mexico City. It is still too early to say whether the increased voting for the opposition party represents a trend away from the PRI, the dominant political party. Most likely, this voting pattern is a specific response to a specific situation that could be reversed by a variety of factors, including better economic management by the government, reduced corruption, and policies that are successful in stimulating economic growth.

The Government and the Private Sector

Related to the discussion of Mexico's middle class is the issue of private-sector confidence in the government. The relationship between the Mexican government and the private sector has never been an easy one, in part because the private sector was "on the wrong side" during the Mexican Revolution. More relevant, however, is the fact that the political system established in the aftermath of the revolution incorporated political groups with very different conceptions of the role that the government should play in the economy. These groups also disagreed on the importance and value of the private sector for Mexico's economic development.

In its most simplified form, this issue is basically divided between two groups within the government. Both claim to accept the idea that Mexico should have a mixed economy, with both the state and the private sector playing complementary roles in Mexico's development efforts. But the first group is essentially statist in its orientation. It believes that the government should play a large and dynamic role within the Mexican economy, including state ownership and/or control of basic and often not-so-basic industries. The private sector, in contrast, should play a secondary and in many ways reactive role, accepting and complementing the state's development endeavors. The statists have a rather low opinion of the private sector, tending to regard it as inefficient, corrupt, parasitic, and interested mainly in profits rather than in the greater good of Mexico. The statists' view of the state, on the other hand, is very positive. They regard it as efficient, productive, and concerned about the general welfare of the majority of Mexicans. The other group within the government holds almost diametrically opposed views. It tends to see the state as inefficient, corrupt, parasitic, and interested more in playing politics than in spurring economic growth, whereas it views the private sector as efficient, productive, and honest. Not surprisingly, this latter group believes that the role of the state in the economy should be decreased and that the private sector should be supported and strengthened.

Despite this split within the government, business and government generally have worked well together. Clark Reynolds has characterized this mutually beneficial relationship as an "alliance for profits." Nevertheless, there have been periods of substantial conflict between the public and private sectors. These have occurred when the government has been under pressure from other groups in society, particularly the labor movement, or when the economy has not performed well enough to allow the government to meet the important demands that organized political groups are making upon it. During such periods, the statists within the government charge that the "development model is not working" and should therefore be changed through an expansion of the role of the state in the economy. But when the government moves in this direction, business-government relations tend to deteriorate further, ultimately obliging the government to make amends to the private sector and to signal clearly that the private sector can and will continue to play an important role in the Mexican economy and receive government support in order to do so.

Business-government relations began to deteriorate during the administration of Luís Echeverría Alvarez, who, within the Mexican political context, was considered a populist. Although the private sector continued to profit economically from Echeverría's policies, his attempts to change the economic and political rules of the game in Mexico (which included encouraging the growth of the so-called independent unions and the breaking of labor contracts that had already been concluded) caused apprehension and anger within the private sector. President José López Portillo, Echeverría's successor, initially tried to calm the fears of the private sector. His success was short-lived, however, as a result of his gross mismanagement of the Mexican economy and his unexpected expropriation of the banks. Both developments brought business-government relations in Mexico to their lowest point in decades.

Put simply, the private sector has lost much of its confidence and trust in Mexico's political leaders. A great deal of effort will be required to restore both. President Míguel de la Madrid Hurtado has made some progress in this regard. His handling of the debt crisis, Mexico's successful implementation to date of an IMF-approved austerity program, and the resumption of at least some economic growth have contributed to improving business-government relations. But much remains to be done. The government, for example, is still sending out mixed signals concerning its attitude toward foreign investment. Many private-sector firms continue to find it difficult to survive and prosper, largely because of the severe restrictions on imports and the shortage of money resulting in part from Mexico's austerity program. If the Mexican economy continues to recover and the de la Madrid administration continues its efforts to regain the confidence of the private sector, government and business could once again cooperate in a mutually beneficial relationship. But the restoration of such a relationship is far from certain at this point.

The Anticorruption Campaign

The anticorruption campaign of the de la Madrid administration is relevant to the government's efforts to restore and enhance its credibility, not only with the private sector but also with the middle class in general. Corruption reached unprecedented heights during the López Portillo administration—probably because there was more money in the system as a result of the oil boom. The de la Madrid administration has committed itself to reducing corruption, in part because it would be very difficult to implement an austerity program if people doubted the honesty of their government officials. The anticorruption campaign is therefore a necessary part of the government's efforts to put the Mexican economy in order.

Unfortunately, however, the anticorruption campaign is potentially risky politically. Duing a time of economic crisis, Mexico's political elites must draw together if Mexico is to be able to deal with the political tensions that are being generated by the economic crisis—but the anticorruption campaign has the potential for splitting the elites. Too zealous a campaign could reach too high into the political system and cause Mexico's political leaders to quarrel among themselves. President de la Madrid thus has the difficult task of taking enough action against corruption so as to convince Mexican voters (particularly among the middle class) that he is serious while not going so far as to undermine political unity. To date, action has been taken against some high-level officials, and there does seem to have been a decrease in the perceived level of corruption in the country. Whether this is a result of Mexico's economic crisis and the adoption of an austerity program or the result of the administration's anticorruption campaign (or both) remains unclear.

Mexico and the Central American Crisis

The anticorruption campaign is not the only development that comes at a bad time for Mexico: The crisis in Central America, too, would have been more manageable for Mexico were it not for the economic crisis. The reasons are as follows. First, the Mexican government rejects the so-called domino theory of the Reagan administration, which asserts that all Central American countries as well as Mexico are vulnerable to political destabilization by Marxist guerrillas. Mexico argues that it is more developed than the countries of Central America and has a more responsive political system. Both factors make it less vulnerable to revolution than its small, poor neighbors to the south. Second, Mexico has already had a revolution, and many Mexicans seem to believe that once a country has had a revolution, a second revolution is impossible. Third, the Mexican government argues that even if Marxist governments were to come to power throughout Central America, Mexico's political stability would not be threatened. The reason is that Mexico would establish friendly relations with such governments and, as a result, would not work to weaken or overthrow the Mexican political system. Mexico bases this argument on the fact that it has established a good working relationship with the Cuban government, despite the fact that Cuba's government is Marxist and Mexico's is not. Mexico is also influenced by the Mexican government's success in co-opting rebel groups that have operated within Mexico.

If Mexico were not undergoing an economic crisis, events in Central America probably would have a minimal effect on the country. But the existence of the economic crisis does not mean that the events in Central America must necessarily threaten Mexico's political stability. It does mean, however, that Mexico is more vulnerable to the impact of events in Central America than Mexico's leaders have been willing to acknowledge publicly.

One obvious impact of the Central American crisis is the influx of large numbers of refugees across Mexico's southern border. Some estimates place their number as high as 100,000, but the accuracy of this or any other figure is difficult to ascertain. These refugees are entering Mexico's poorest region, one already populated by Indians whose standard of living often appears to differ little from that of the refugees before they fled their countries. The entry into southern Mexico of large numbers of displaced persons who require food, shelter, and employment has begun to exacerbate the problems of an area already beset by severe socioeconomic problems. It has also created a security problem, inasmuch as some of the refugees are Marxist guerrillas. Although it denies this fact publicly, the Mexican government has begun to move the refugee camps away from the border and further into the Mexican interior—an action that can be interpreted as tacit acknowledgment of guerrilla infiltration. Mexico has also reinforced its military forces in the border region. Finally, to deal with the socioeconomic problem, the Mexican government has launched the Plan Chiapas, an ambitious development program aimed at creating employment and improving the standard of living of the population in the area.

Another impact of the Central American crisis on Mexico has been increased political polarization within Mexico, which has occurred primarily because successful revolution in one country, in this case Nicaragua, tends to encourage optimism and increased activism among revolutionaries in nearby countries. At the same time, it has frightened the economic elites in the same countries. The result has been a weakening of the political center. This is what began to happen in Mexico in the immediate aftermath of the Cuban Revolution. In the early 1960s, however, the Mexican economy was growing rapidly, thereby making it easier for Mexico's political leaders to co-opt or destroy guerrillas on the left and to pursue additional policies to restore confidence on the right.

Mexico today has no active and important guerrilla movement. Furthermore, the economic crisis has focused both the left and the right on domestic political and economic realities rather than on events to Mexico's south.

Conclusion

On the whole, there is justification for either pessimism or optimism regarding Mexico's future. Under a pessimistic scenario, oil prices would continue to decline precipitously, interest rates would increase substantially, the U.S. economy would enter into a severe recession, or any combination of these three events would occur. Any or all of these developments would seriously undermine Mexico's incipient economic recovery. Moreover, political tensions would increase, and the Mexican government might feel forced to relax its austerity program and perhaps resort to anti-American rhetoric or actions in order to deal with rising discontent within Mexico. In the worst-case scenario, such actions might even fail to prevent a more serious crisis within Mexico.

The more optimistic scenario posits slow but continued improvement of the Mexican economy, in part as a result of continued improvement in the U.S. economy and the international economic environment. The resumption of economic growth would not only deflate the sense of crisis somewhat (as has already happened to a certain extent) but it would also make Mexico's other problems more manageable. The more optimistic scenario seems much more likely at this point.

PART TWO

The Impact of Trade on Mexico's Economy

3

U.S.-Mexico Trade Relations

Guy F. Erb

Introduction

Mexico and the United States share a border, a contentious history, and significant trade, financial, and other ties, but the countries are divided by quite different economic philosophies. For Mexico, reliance on a "mixed market economy" and the overriding importance attached to national development have led to the government's insistence on autonomous trade and investment decisions. Under the impact of the crisis of the 1980s, Mexico has begun to move away from its traditional reliance on import substitution, buttressing domestic policy changes with its accession to the General Agreement on Tariffs and Trade (GATT), which was completed in September 1986. However, Mexico still relies heavily on the "rectorship of the state"; that is, the government assigns itself the role of determining the strategic direction for the Mexican economy.

The U.S. government, on the other hand, has traditionally based its trade policies on a series of international commitments and acceptance of restraints on unilateral actions, particularly the guidelines found in the GATT. Although the United States and other industrialized countries often seek to circumvent GATT rules, the overall commitment to a liberal world trading system—an international marketplace—remains a very significant aspect of U.S. trade policy. The many trade and investment disputes that confront the two nations stem from the different foundation for policy that each has built.

In the highly charged atmosphere of the politico-economic relationship between the countries, trade policy changes by one or the other can be of great significance, sometimes taking on political overtones that ultimately require resolution by heads of state or cabinet officials. Yet the disputes themselves usually revolve around narrowly defined issues or technical matters affecting amounts of trade that are small when compared to the total value of commerce between Mexico and the United States. In Washington these trade cases are seen as the result of a legitimate complaint by the U.S. interests involved and as examples of Mexican practices—whether subsidies, fiscal incentives, or protectionist decrees—that affect entire sectors of the U.S. economy. Hence the seriousness with which the U.S. executive branch, the Congress, and some business and labor interests view the direction of Mexican trade policy.

Mexican Trade Policy

Traditionally, Mexican governments based their trade policies on the premise that national development comes first. Import restrictions, export promotion, and trade and investment performance requirements were intended to sustain economic growth. By promoting this objective with state investment, fiscal measures, and national planning, the Mexican government subordinated the international consequences of its actions to domestic objectives. Thus, Mexico considered its policy autonomy to be of far greater importance than the benefits, which some in Mexico see as dubious, that might be derived from participation in a multilateral framework for trade. Frequent recourse to import restraints, industrial incentives, subsidies, and tax offsets has made Mexico's sovereignty of economic decisionmaking an ever more important aspect of its bilateral trade relations with the United States. The decline in importance of subsidies, import licenses, and tax incentives that occurred during the administration of President de la Madrid, which Mexico's GATT membership ratified, has added a significant dimension to bilateral trade relations. The differences in underlying philosophy that characterized past bilateral trade discussions are not yet resolved completely. However, Mexico's steps toward economic modernization and its new commitment to multilateralism have changed the nature of those discussions. The continuity of the trade policies of de la Madrid is now the central issue for the two countries, rather than the contentious contrast of each country's approach to trade negotiations.

This is not to say that Mexico's trade liberalization and GATT membership will bridge the gap between the negotiators from the highly industrialized United States and those from Mexico, who represent a developing country—albeit one that is "advanced" or "newly industrialized." For officials in Mexico City, national development policies create the opportunities for hundreds of thousands of Mexicans to find employment, develop a market for the products and technology of the United States, and make Mexico a profitable site for foreign direct investment. The migration of workers to the north, whether due to shortfalls in the creation of jobs in Mexico or to the pull of high wages and labor demand in the United States, is viewed officially as a mutually beneficial provision of labor to U.S. firms and farms that illustrates the complementarity of the two work forces.

If confronted with the argument that Mexico's policies have a restrictive impact on trade between the two countries, the Mexican government may still buttress its contention that development policies benefit the U.S. economy by referring to the normally substantial Mexican imports from the United States. But U.S. officials have held that such "implicit" recipocity is not sufficient to ensure the continuation of the relatively open U.S. market for Mexican products without domestic challenge.

Mexico has frequently raised trade issues directly with senior U.S officials, seeking a case-by-case approach to trade disputes in which technical negotiations can be subordinated to the fundamental interests both countries have in the bilateral relationship. Thus reference may be made to

- other aspects of the bilateral relationship (e.g., energy, migration, and fishery questions);
- the impact of Mexican debts on the international financial system; or,
- the close and mutually beneficial economic ties that exist between the United States and Mexico.

Mexico's international debts and its petroleum reserves have placed the country among the most significant of the world's economies. High economic growth until the prolonged crisis of the 1980s set Mexico apart from most developed and developing countries and brought it to the number-three position among U.S. trading partners, a place it lost by 1986. Mexico's natural resources and strong domestic market have induced most major U.S. corporations to invest in subsidiaries or to undertake business with Mexican partners. Northern Mexico and the U.S. Southwest combine to form an area of economic development that rivals the traditional U.S. growth centers.

These factors all contribute to various views about the appropriate relationship between the two countries. Trade and investment policies are certainly the subjects of intense debate in Mexico. Mexico's reliance on earnings from petroleum exports, relatively small exports of manufactures, agricultural shortcomings, and questions about the desirability of continued high emigration, as well as bilateral trade policies, are all topics of concern to policymakers and others in Mexico. However, the centralized nature of the Mexican government fosters a unity of official purpose and policy presentation usually unmatched by the U.S. government. Compared to the open—and seemingly continuous—clash of opinions among the executive branch, Congress, business, and labor that characterizes trade policy in the United States, Mexicans have demonstrated an ability to close ranks once decisions are taken. A recent, although imperfect, illustration of this capacity is found in the GATT accession debate in Mexico. Fierce criticism of the government's proposal preceded the final decision by de la Madrid to pursue GATT membership. Once the die was cast, the disagreements over the policy decision were muted, but firms and business associations scrambled to defer the impact of trade liberalization on their operations.

U.S. Views of Mexican Trade Policy

Some tension exists between Americans who seek a "fairer" (i.e., more directly reciprocal) relationship with Mexico and those who believe that Mexico is important in many ways to the United States, and who therefore seek amicable trade relations, even if that requires nonreciprocal concessions or postponement of dispute settlement. The proponents of the first school of thought would let particular trade cases take their course with little or no reference to either the broad bilateral relationship or other factors that might be expected to improve trade relations. To illustrate, U.S. interests seeking reciprocity with Mexico in the area of intellectual property carried their viewpoint to high U.S. policy circles even in the period immediately after Mexico's accession to the GATT. That major multilateral trade initiative by Mexico did not halt efforts in 1986 by research-intensive industries and by U.S. negotiators to obtain concessions on patent protection from Mexican authorities.

Those who would put trade and investment in the context of overall U.S.-Mexico relations emphasize the interdependence of economic and political issues and consequently search for smooth resolution of trade disputes. This position has become harder to sustain in U.S. government policy circles. The overwhelming concern over the U.S. trade deficit, when combined with the complaints of U.S. industries, frequently outweighs objections on foreign policy grounds to U.S. trade restrictions.

Adherents of each viewpoint are found in all the constituencies that influence trade policy. The executive branch, the Congress, and the business community reflect both tendencies; organized labor tends to identify with the first school. The U.S. decisionmaking process is fragmented, with centers of power distributed throughout the government and the private sector. On occasion, U.S. trade policy toward Mexico has not enjoyed a consensus of support for a particular direction, and specific issues have been settled according to the weight that each constituency has exerted over the decision at hand.

The Executive Branch

U.S. trade policy officials are resigned to spending weeks on end wrestling with issues posed by imports of clothespins from China, footwear from Korea, or steel from Mexico. Tempers flare from time to time, but the trade policy community sees such import conflicts as events that derive from complaints from individual firms, unions, or agricultural interests rather than as manifestations of centrally directed policies against other countries. Broad policy objectives (e.g., the liberalization of the Japanese trading regime or Mexican adherence to the GATT) can be and usually are separated from specific cases. This compartmentalization occurs even if, in American eyes, the case may illustrate the need for the broad policy change that the United States seeks from another nation.

Trade policy officials attempt to treat trade policy complaints individually. This is the case particularly because trade officials know that their decision on a complaint about Mexican subsidies or Japanese autos may be challenged in court or criticized in Congress, perhaps to the point that official action or inaction will provoke the introduction of legislation. U.S. trade officials and negotiators also try to minimize the impact of other aspects of a bilateral relationship on their policies, insofar as they fear that their leverage over trade issues will be weakened if they or other officials show sensitivity to concerns outside the trade area (e.g., U.S. access to Mexican energy resources in the case of a subsidy ruling on an import from Mexico).

Despite the desire of trade negotiators to maximize their bargaining leverage, and despite the statutory requirements that trade matters be resolved without reference to outside influences, some interests in the government and the private sector may argue for favorable resolution of U.S.-Mexican trade disputes on the grounds of the overall bilateral relationship. This constituency may be stronger in one agency or another in different administrations, or may see its influence reduced by U.S.-Mexico foreign policy differences. However, the importance to the United States of its economic and financial links to Mexico ensures that this faction will be represented in any policy debate on bilateral trade.

In President Carter's administration, the association between the State Department and the Office of the Special Coordinator for Mexico (the creation of which was itself an attempt to signal to the bureaucracy the importance of Mexico to the United States) reinforced the State Department's sensitivity to foreign policy concerns in the consideration of trade issues with Mexico. It proved difficult, however, to forge an effective link between the coordinator and trade policymakers. In the Reagan administration, the Commerce Department initially reflected

President Reagan's desire to establish a good working relationship with President Miguel de la Madrid Hurtado, as indicated by the secretary of commerce's attempts to devise a complaint about imports of toy balloons from Mexico.[1]

By 1986, however, concerns over the U.S. trade deficit, congressional proposals to protect the U.S. economy from overseas competition, and persistent U.S. doubts about certain aspects of Mexico's trade and investment regime offset the Reagan administration's early sensitivity to Mexico's difficulties during its economic crisis.

Public and congressional reaction to the toy balloon case and to Mexican export subsidies clearly illustrated the tension between those who seek a reciprocal relationship with Mexico and others who want to promote "good" bilateral policies. To those in the executive branch who deal with Mexico on such issues as the conflicts in Central America, complaints about subsidies on toy balloons, leather wear, or tiles may seem to be diversions from the "high policy" issues that should occupy the leaders of two such important neighboring countries. Nevertheless, those seeking reciprocal concessions push on: Neither the drop in oil prices (and the consequent worsening of Mexico's external accounts and debt service capacity) nor GATT membership were sufficient to blunt the U.S. drive in 1986 for changes in Mexican laws on patents and trademarks.

The Congress

The possibility of action by individual senators or representatives, or of the passage of new trade legislation, exerts a pervasive influence over executive branch trade policies. The toy balloon case cited above illustrates the point. Senator John Heinz (R., Pa.) wrote to Commerce Secretary Malcolm Baldrige to express his "concern and disappointment" over what he saw as a "serious disregard" for U.S. trade laws in the Department of Commerce ruling.[2] Senator Heinz also introduced a bill that would have set conditions so strictly defining "countries under the agreement" (the Multilateral Trade Negotiations [MTN] subsidies code) that U.S. negotiators would have had an even more formidable task in seeking Mexico's adherence to the code.[3]

Senators Heinz and Daniel P. Moynihan (D., N.Y.) also submitted a bill that would have given the president authority to remove U.S. tariff preferences from countries that employed investment performance requirements, such as the Mexican Automotive Decree. In addition, the bill would have tightened up the U.S. ability to extend tariff preferences in ways that would have been adverse to Mexican exports of manufactures.[4] Another example of congressional responses to Mexican trade and investment policies is found in the persistent exhortations by certain senators to the U.S. trade representative (USTR) to "be tough" in the negotiations with Mexico regarding intellectual property.[5]

Mexico's industrial policies have also come under fire in the U.S. Congress. A case in 1983-1984 involved congressional reaction to a U.S. Department of Commerce decision that Mexico's pricing of natural gas did not represent a subsidy to the production and export of anhydrous ammonia.[6] Natural gas is the feedstock for that product, and domestic prices in Mexico are below the price of its natural gas exports to the United States. In reaction to the ruling, Senator Russell Long (D., La.) and Representative Sam Gibbons (D., Fla.) supported legislative changes in U.S. trade laws that would define such pricing practices as a countervailable subsidy.[7] The early congressional action in this case was clearly related to the absence of a negotiated agreement between the United States and Mexico that committed each country to certain norms, especially Mexican observance of the standards set in the Code on Subsidies and Countervailing Duties. However, even after Mexico had signed a subsidies agreement with the United States, pressure continued from certain quarters for restrictions on energy-intensive exports from Mexico. The House passed restrictions on "natural resource imput subsidies" during the 99th Congress.[8] Moreover, in 1986, the Commerce Department, in response to an International Trade Court ruling as well as to congressional concerns, issued preliminary interpretations of trade laws that may allow wider applications of countervailing duties to Mexico's energy intensive exports.[9]

Thus, despite executive branch intentions toward Mexico, or other countries, the U.S. Congress may assert its own trade policy objectives at any time, regardless of the consequences for bilateral relations with specific countries. Some members of Congress are genuinely concerned about the direction of U.S. trade policies toward developing countries, the challenges to GATT from the policies of the advanced developing countries (including Mexico), and the need to implement the codes agreed to in the MTN. This group would resist any tendency by the executive branch to make exceptions for Mexico. Others in the Congress represent districts that have seen the effects of competition with Mexico, and their tolerance for Mexico's protective encouragement of its industries is very low.

Senators and representatives hear frequently from their constituents about Mexican barriers to trade between the two countries. Moreover, congressional attitudes toward Mexico have been adversely affected by the frequent changes in the Mexican import regime. For example, the Mexican authorities intended that the significant increase in import license requirements in mid-1981 would help them overcome the increase in Mexico's current account deficit that resulted from a drop in oil export revenues. However, although it was understandable from a Mexican point of view, the magnitude of the increase in protection and the abruptness of the move caused considerable resentment in congressional circles.

Institutional memories are shorter in the United States than in Mexico, particularly since the relationship is asymmetrical. Remembrance of the impact on Mexico of a comparable U.S. action, the 10 percent import surcharge of 1971, does not temper congressional reactions to Mexico's trade policies. Although Mexico's GATT membership might have been expected to offset negative feelings about Mexico's trade and investment regimes, the hoped for result did not occur in mid-1986. Instead, concerns about the trade deficit and the disagreement over intellectual property largely offset whatever negotiating gains Mexico could have realized from its accession to the GATT.

Such factors reinforce the impact of the usually small group of representatives and senators who follow U.S.-Mexican trade relations closely. As in most issues before the Congress, such a small group has a disproportionate impact on the outcome of most policy debates because the majority of their colleagues tend to follow their lead. It is a rare elected representative who will take a stand against the expressed wishes of a powerful constituent, even when it can be argued that such a stand would meet the broad U.S. objective of good bilateral relations with Mexico.

Business and Labor

Attitudes toward Mexico among various private U.S. constituencies depend heavily on their degree of involvement with Mexico. Most unions feel threatened by the low wages paid to an increasingly skilled Mexican work force. Leaders of organized labor in the United States consequently find themselves in opposition to current Mexican trade policy and to any U.S. tendency to accommodate it.[10] They advocate reciprocity, graduation, and, if necessary, retaliatory legislation and executive action to counter what they see as unfair trade and industrial measures. Firms that face competition from Mexico may also associate themselves with this view. Many have brought specific complaints against what they claim are subsidies to Mexican exports. By early 1984 such complaints had made Mexico the target of numerous complaints that resulted in the imposition of countervailing duties against Mexican subsidies.

The crisis of 1982-1983 and the nationalization of the banks shook the confidence in Mexico's market of many U.S. companies, especially major corporations with investments in Mexico. The problems posed by Mexican trade and investment policies receive careful scrutiny as business leaders assess the challenges and opportunities in Mexico. Assertive trade, investment, and technology policies, seen before the crisis as the logical consequence of doing business in an advanced developing country, are now regarded in some business sectors as fit subjects of reciprocal government-to-government negotiation.

The caution that now characterizes corporate attitudes is accompanied by questions about the Mexican planners who are attempting to upgrade the skills and employment of the Mexican work force, to overcome the highly centralized nature of the Mexican economy, and to develop new industrial sectors in Mexico. Some U.S. corporate representatives have spoken approvingly of the flexibility of Mexico's investment policies and note that the Mexican government does not present its plans as rigid blueprints. Others object to the lack of certainty and the red tape that characterize Mexican responses to requests for authorizations of investment plans.

Still other firms, which entered Mexico under "market reserve" arrangements that protect small-scale, inefficient operations from foreign competition, are now pleading with the government for more time to adapt to the new rules of the game under Mexico's liberalized trade regime. Nevertheless, the success of Mexico's industrialization, employment, and export policies would serve the long-term interests of international companies. Even among those U.S. industrial sectors that would experience competition from Mexican exports it is possible to find firms that prefer to view Mexico as an economic partner. Criticism of Mexican policies or support for restrictive U.S. legislation will thus remain tempered by the appreciation of Mexico as a site for profitable enterprise, particularly if the Mexican economy recovers from the stop-and-go policies that have limited its growth in the 1980s.

At the same time, a significant part of business and labor has registered serious concern about the trade barriers created by Mexico's performance requirements: Import-substitution goals seem to have the same effects as import quotas or licensing, and export promotion seems equivalent to export subsidies. The absence of any international discipline (or even informal ground rules) governing such policies gives rise to additional worry about the impact of such policies on long-run U.S. interests.[11] The Labor-Industry Coalition for International Trade (LICIT) is one body that represents this point of view. In addition to opposing performance requirements, LICIT supports the graduation of advanced developing countries from preferential tariff treatment. However, LICIT's initial criticism of performance requirements was toned down by an AFL-CIO decision to seek local content requirements for investments in the United States.

LICIT's labor position regarding local content requirements led this coalition to concentrate on criticizing export performance requirements abroad; among these was the Automotive Decree, the most prominent Mexican performance requirement.[12] Any criticism of this decree, however, confronts the two pillars of Mexican trade policy: sovereignty and nonreciprocity. The Mexican government considers the Automotive Decree as a non-negotiable item, on the grounds that it was an autonomous policy decision and that the relatively open U.S. market for Mexican exports of automotive parts is so obviously in the interest of both countries that Mexico should not be asked to alter the decree as a means of keeping the U.S. market open. The Ford Motor Company's decision in 1984 to invest $500 million in Mexico strengthened the Mexican response.

It is in the nature of U.S. trade policy that specific complaints can be presented to the executive branch and to the courts without regard to their impact on the foreign policy, security, or commercial interests that may exist between the United States and its trading partners. To illustrate, one need only point to the conflicts over everything from chickens to steel with the Europeans. Under the principle that "the squeaky wheel gets the grease," we can expect the complaints about auto parts, subsidized Mexican exports, and other matters to gain more and more attention in the United States.

Despite the evident concern of U.S. banks and many corporations about the development of Mexico's economy and Mexican exports, they are unlikely to enter a trade policy dispute on behalf of Mexico unless their own interests are directly involved. In the context of the global effort to liberalize the world markets that began in Uruguay in 1986, it may be possible to forestall calls for protection of U.S. markets, even when foreign practices coincide with painful industrial adjustment in the United States. The Uruguay Round of multilateral trade negotiations will not halt complaints about the impact on U.S. firms and labor of Mexican exports—a fact that will keep both U.S. private and official supporters of greater bilateral trade on the defensive.

Trade Negotiations Between Mexico and the United States

For the past several years the United States has experienced a major transformation of its domestic industry. The decline in output and employment of the "smokestack" industries in the midwestern and northeastern United States has been offset only in part by the production of new goods and services. Regional and sectoral disparities in growth mean that demands for protection, which were strongest during the recession of 1981-1982, have persisted during the economic recovery. Furthermore, until 1986 the strong dollar put many industrial sectors in the United States under competitive pressure in both domestic and foreign markets. In addition, labor unions, having made numerous wage and benefit concessions during the recession, are not disposed to accept what they regard as unfair foreign competition from direct or indirect government subsidies to export industries.

Frequently called for in the Congress, therefore, are tighter administration of U.S. trade laws, new, tougher trade legislation, and reciprocal bargaining with advanced developing countries. The Reagan administration's decisions to restrict imports of steel, textiles, and other products were made in response to such pressures. But the need for reciprocity was already a recurring theme in the 1981 private business presentations to the U.S. government in connection with North American trade agreements.[13] (Service industries, particularly trucking, were singled out. In response to perceived inequality of treatment—a perception that arose as a result of the deregulation of the U.S. trucking industry— U.S. government agencies supported private calls for fully reciprocal treatment of U.S. truckers before Mexican carriers could receive permits to operate in the United States.)[14] Broader calls for reciprocity have figured prominently in U.S. trade policy debates since then.

Mexico has been singled out as a prime example of a country from which U.S. negotiators should seek a more reciprocal relationship.[15] The Office of the U.S. Trade Representative sees reciprocal bargaining with Mexico and other developing countries as essential to sustaining U.S. trade initiatives toward these countries. For example, the executive branch proposals in 1984 to prolong the U.S. Generalized System of Preferences (GSP)—originally conceived as a nonreciprocal, duty-free program for developing countries—included strong inducements to Mexico and other advanced developing nations to negotiate on trade with the United States.[16] However, the proposed changes in the preference system (e.g., graduation of many products from the main beneficiaries and the link between access to preferences and trade liberalization) did not defuse strong criticism of the requested ten-year extension of the U.S. tariff preferences.[17] Moreover, the approval of the GSP included provisions for negotiations with beneficiary countries that, in Mexico's case, led to the dispute over intellectual property and to the withdrawal of some GSP benefits in 1987, under authority of the Trade Act of 1984.

U.S. trade negotiators have been seeking signs of a long-term Mexican commitment to a more open trade regime and to export-led growth. Although various Mexican government and industrial interests appear reluctant to break with the inward-looking, import-substitution development policies that Mexico has followed since the 1940s, some progress has been achieved by the two governments on measures to reduce trade frictions. Their efforts concentrated on Mexico's desire to achieve an agreement that would allow Mexican exports to receive an injury test before the United States imposed countervailing duties to offset Mexican subsidies. After a long period during which countervailing duties were only infrequently imposed on Mexican exports,[18] a rash of complaints in the early 1980s led to numerous countervailing duties and to renewed efforts to resolve that long-standing trade dispute. These negotiations were narrowly drawn and did not address the other trade policy concerns of both countries or the alternatives that multilateral or broader bilateral trade talks would provide to them. The GATT accession negotiations opened the door to multilateral bargaining.

Multilateral Negotiations

Frequently, Mexico and the United States have differed over the appropriate framework for their mutual trade. Since the formation of the Bretton Woods institutions and the General Agreement on Tariffs and Trade, the United States has been an advocate of multilateralism. Until it acceded to the GATT in 1986, Mexico maintained an independent trade policy, preferring to resolve disputes that arise in the United States in bilateral, not multilateral, consultations. With this accession, Mexico opened a new chapter in its relations with the United States and its other trade partners.

Mexico participated actively in the Multilateral Trade Negotiations of the 1970s but decided not to implement the MTN's exchange of tariff concessions and its codes to govern the use of subsidies and countervailing duties as well as other trade policy instruments. Mexico later signed an agreement with the United States on subsidies that brought it into compliance with the guidelines of the subsidies codes. At the Punta del Este talks that launched the Uruguay Round, Mexico was active in the moderate group of developing countries that opposed Brazilian and Indian efforts to limit the scope of the new MTN. Further evidence of Mexico's multilateral initiatives was provided by its negotiations with Argentina, Brazil, and Uruguay in a renewed attempt to create a Latin American trade agreement.[19]

The U.S. government continues to advocate multilateral solutions to the trade problems of the 1980s and hopes to give significant momentum to a new multilateral round of trade negotiations, including issues of direct interest to developing countries. Thus, the option of participation in a new, multilateral round of global trade negotiations that would also include north/south trade bargaining is open to Mexico and the United

States. U.S.-Mexico negotiations within a multilateral framework would be tangible evidence of a commitment by the two countries to seek a mutual liberalization of trade and could also restrain calls in the United States for trade barriers against Mexican products.

Multilateral trade negotiations are lengthy affairs. The framers of the Uruguay Round of trade negotiations set a four-year time limit, but even with that self-imposed discipline, the Round's benefits will probably be phased over a five- or ten-year period. Thus, direct and near-term benefits from the current multilateral negotiations will be limited to the restrains imposed on new barriers to trade. The Uruguay Round of negotiations will not create a certain framework for U.S.-Mexico trade, nor will they resolve the many trade issues that already confront Mexico and the United States.

Bilateral Trade Negotiations

Despite its traditional advocacy of multilateralism, the U.S. government took steps in the mid-1980s that revealed a willingness to negotiate regional or bilateral trade arrangements. Those steps included trade preferences granted within the Caribbean Basin Initiative, successful negotiations with Israel on a bilateral free trade area, and commencement of negotiations with Canada on a free trade area and with Mexico on a framework for bilateral trade.

Bilateral measures may well respond best to the policy directions of the U.S. and Mexican governments. Whatever lies ahead on the multilateral front will surely take a long time to develop, whereas bilateral negotiations can promptly address issues whose resolution would improve the trade prospects of both countries. Moreover, the absence of an agreed framework for trade deprives exporters and investors in each country of the certainty that could lead to commercial exchanges that are even greater than those currently maintained by the two countries.

If they are to make significant long-run contributions to the development of both countries, bilateral arrangements need to foster the efficient employment of capital, workers, and natural resources. If too narrowly drawn, bilateral measures could limit rather than enhance the economic growth of the two countries. However, well-designed bilateral cooperation could bring the two countries out of the time-consuming and trade-inhibiting case-by-case approach they now follow. They could thus substitute bilaterally negotiated agreements and safeguards for the current disputes over unilaterally imposed policies and trade restrictions. Negotiations to reach such agreements could either take place on a sector-by-sector or regional basis[20] or aim at a broad, overarching commercial accord.

To be politically viable in the United States, a bilateral agreement of either type would have to involve mutual commitments and an exchange of concessions. In other words, Mexico would make an appropriate, but not symmetrical, offer in exchange for trade policy commitments by the United States. While they were in progress, sectoral or broad bilateral negotiations would in themselves restrain efforts to impose new restrictions on Mexican exports. Neither sectoral talks nor efforts to reach a bilateral commercial accord would preclude negotiations by the two countries in a multilateral framework.

Sectoral Agreements. Bilateral negotiations can free up trade within specific industrial sectors. For instance, the U.S.-Canadian automotive pact is a preferential agreement that required a GATT waiver. The United States and Canada discussed additional sectoral agreements in 1983 and 1984, but U.S. and Mexican officials have considered only in a preliminary manner the possibility of sectoral talks.

Sectoral negotiations could help resolve U.S.-Mexican differences in the automotive, steel, and other sectors, where Mexican industrial policies are the subject of some disagreements (e.g., in the pharmaceutical and computer industries). Labor and industry in both countries face difficult adjustments to changing technologies, the requirements of developing strong export industries, and competition from other countries. Sectoral agreements could ease the adjustment process of both countries. Sectoral accords could be based on an exchange of most-favored-nation concessions, perhaps directed at products pertaining to which the two countries would be the most likely beneficiaries of trade liberalization. The alternative, preferential agreements, would be subject to approval by the GATT, insofar as the United States was concerned. Sectoral agreements could also be designed to take account of the disparities between the two countries, given that, as the Canadian automotive agreement shows, the smaller of the trading parties can benefit significantly from the growth of total commerce within the target sector. There are some drawbacks to the sectoral approach, however. The concentration on one sector may pit competitors against one another, thus heightening tensions and eliminating the prospects for trade-offs across sectors that sustain broader negotiations. Moreover, the narrow focus of sectoral negotiations may lengthen the time necessary to achieve truly significant trade liberalization.

A Broad Commercial Accord. Mexico and the United States could negotiate a commercial agreement based on shared principles and mutual commitments to dispute settlement.[21] The starting points for the two countries would be the definition of their common development and commercial objectives; a commitment to adhere to policies consistent with those objectives, including the appropriate use of subsidies; agreement on timely communication of intentions; and procedures for the resolution of differences.

The definition of common goals and the commitment to act consistently with them would move both nations toward a framework of principles and rules that would provide the stability needed by private risk-takers in both nations in order to function effectively. Such a framework would help determine where business could expect to operate profitably in each country and would thus encourage long-term commitments of private resources to trade and investment. It may also provide the backdrop to sector-by-sector trade liberalization.

The establishment of common purposes by the two governments would generate a set of expectations regarding the official and private sectors in both nations. Trade policy officials would therefore face checkpoints that would hinder measures likely to harm the other country's interests. The assessment of policy initiatives before their introduction in relation to those checkpoints would help avoid conflicts and could also promote the gradual increase of shared objectives.

Eventually, a broad commercial accord could include agreements on such key issues as subsidies, countervailing duties, import licensing, incentives and performance requirements that affect trade, and investment policies. Such an accord was actively considered by business groups in both countries during 1982–1984 and has also been the subject of preliminary government-to-government consultations.

Key Trade Issues

The U.S. and Mexican governments have long adhered to broadly stated policy positions that make it difficult for them to contemplate the concessions and compromises that would underpin a viable bilateral accord. However, the increasing number of trade conflicts may prompt officials in both nations to reexamine the premises and attitudes that have led to the current trade policy situation.

Serious bargaining on a bilateral agreement would entail a willingness on the part of both governments to consider some fundamental trade-offs. For example, U.S. officials would have to accept that a bilateral agreement would be a modification of the emphasis on multilateralism that has marked post–World War II U.S. trade policy. Likewise, Mexican officials would have to accept that the commitments made in the negotiation would involve some constraints on their policy autonomy.

U.S. policies have long been based on a multilateral approach to the trade-liberalization and problem-solving measures embodied in the GATT. The commitment to most-favored-nation treatment is still a cornerstone of the GATT and one from which Mexico has received substantial benefits in the form of tariff reductions by the United States and other countries. Although the MFN concept has been bent by special provisions for developing countries and members of economic integration groupings, as well as by the introduction (in 1979) of trade costs whose benefits are limited to code signatories, MFN remains at the center of the multilateral approach to trade that the United States emphasizes. Hence it is unlikely that at this stage of the bilateral relationship a framework agreement would contain discriminatory provisions. If such were the case, a waiver from the GATT for the bilateral agreement would not be necessary.

Congressional approval would also be necessary for any U.S.-Mexico trade agreement, whether or not formal legislation was required. The congressional interest in an agreement that includes the results of fair bargaining with Mexico would make continual consultations with congressional leaders an essential part of the negotiating process. Those consultations would ensure that an executive agreement would not be criticized on Capitol Hill. It would also smooth the way for any legislation that might be required.

For its part, Mexico would have to continue to recognize (as it did in the GATT accession negotiations), that its energy exports to the United States and its imports of capital goods and agricultural staples are not adequate measures of reciprocity for the trade concessions that the United States might make to Mexico. As a heavily indebted developing country, Mexico does operate at a disadvantage in its international transactions, particularly those with the United States. Consequently, Mexico deserves some "special and differential" treatment by the United States and other industrial countries. Still, that fact cannot absolve the Mexican negotiators from putting appropriate trade policy commitments on the bargaining table.

For bilateral negotiations to succeed, each side must seek from the other commitments that are substantial, enforceable, and therefore durable. An exchange of concessions that is meaningless in trade terms would be an exercise in futility for countries whose economic interdependence is so important. Both countries must be satisfied that the agreement provides a stimulus to trade as well as a means of reviewing the actions of the other.

The assessment of the costs and benefits of any form of trade agreement would take place in various political sectors in each nation. In the United States, those who advocate "reciprocal" or "fair" trade relations with Mexico (i.e., those who support rigorous enforcement of U.S. trade laws, countermeasures to offset Mexico's subsidies and performance requirements, and the "graduation" of Mexican products off the GSP list) will be most rigorous in their review of the agreement. There is, nevertheless, a willingness to compromise in the bargaining over trade matters because of Mexico's importance to both the U.S. economy and national security considerations. In evaluating a trade agreement with Mexico, each U.S. constituency would have to weigh the potential results of the negotiation with Mexico in light of the economic, financial, and foreign policy dimensions of the U.S.-Mexico relationship. With the outcome of a serious negotiation to work with, those favoring a durable framework for U.S.-Mexican trade could achieve its approval by the U.S. political system.

Notes

In preparing this article I have drawn on my working paper for the Overseas Development Council's U.S.-Mexico Project, "America's View of Mexican Trade Policies"; on a discussion paper prepared for the U.S.-Mexico Business Leaders Colloquium, Mexico City; and on my work with Robert Herzstein, chairman of the U.S.-Mexico Bilateral Trade Agreement Subcommittee, U.S.-Mexico Business Committee. I am very grateful to all those who have commented on the earlier drafts, but I accept full responsibility for the contents of this article.

1. See Department of Commerce, International Trade Administration, "Toy Balloon and Playballs from Mexico; Dismissal of Countervailing Duty Petition," 46 *Federal Regulation* 31698, Washington, D.C., Wednesday, June 17, 1981; and "Commerce Criticized on Countervailing Duty Case," *Legal Times of Washington,* July 20, 1981.

2. Letter from John Heinz, U.S. Senate, to the Honorable Malcolm Baldridge, Secretary of Commerce, June 19, 1981.

3. *Congressional Record,* July 23, 1981, p. S8302.

4. *Congressional Record,* May 8, 1981, p. S4643.

5. "Senators Want to Repeal GSP benefits if Mexico Fails to Protect Patents," *Inside Washington Trade,* Washington, D.C., October 3, 1986, p. 7.

6. See Department of Commerce, International Trade Administration, "Anhydrous and Aqua Ammonia from Mexico (Final Negative Countervailing Duty Determination)," 48 *Federal Regulation* 28522, Washington, D.C., June 22, 1983. See also Richard C. Rivers, P.C., and Elizabeth C. Seastrum of Akin, Gump, Strauss, Hauer & Feld, "Countervailing Duty Petition Under the Tariff Act of 1930, as Amended, 19 U.S.C. 1303, In the matter of Anhydrous Ammonia from Mexico," Washington, D.C., October 28, 1982.

7. Subcommittee on Trade, Committee on Ways and Means, U.S. House of Representatives, "The Hon. Sam M. Gibbons (D., Fla.), Chairman, Subcommittee on Trade Committee on Ways and Means, Announces Action on Proposals to Improve Statutory Remedies Against Injurious Foreign Subsidies and Dumping," Washington, D.C., September 27, 1983.

8. 99th Congress, 2nd Session, H.R.4800, A bill to enhance the competitiveness of American industry; and for other purposes, May 9, 1986, Section 135, Resource Input Subsidies.

9. "Commerce Decision on Lumber Reveals New Subsidies Interpretations," *Inside U.S. Trade,* Washington, D.C., October 24, 1986, pp. 14–15.

10. Brian Turner and Catherine Bocskor, "United States–Mexico Trade and Investment Relations: Are There any Rules? A Labor Perspective," *Working Paper no. 9,* Overseas Development Council U.S.-Mexico Project, Washington, D.C., July 1982.

11. The Labor-Industry Coalition for International Trade, *Performance Requirements,* Washington, D.C., March 1981.

12. See D.C. Bennett and K. E. Sharpe, "Transnational Corporations, Export Promotion Policies and U.S.-Mexican Automotive Trade," Woodrow Wilson International Center, Washington, D.C., September 18, 1981, mimeo., p. 48; and Alejandro Violante Morlock, "A Critical Juncture in the U.S. Mexican Trade Relationship: The Automotive Sector," *Working Paper no. 3,* Overseas Development Council U.S.-Mexico Project, Washington, D.C., May 1982.

13. Office of the U.S. Trade Representative, "North American Trade Agreements," Study mandated in Section 1104 of the Trade Agreements Act of 1979, July 26, 1981.

14. See Interventions by the Departments of State, Commerce, and Transportation filed with the Interstate Commerce Commission, ICC Dockets MC-141313-1, Sub. no. 1, May-June 1981.

15. Two reports in early 1982 illustrated U.S. government attitudes toward the United States' trade relations with two of its top three trading partners, Mexico and Japan. See William Chislett, "Washington Loses Patience with Mexico," *Financial Times* (London), February 1, 1982; and Robert J. Samuelson, "Japan's Consciousness," *National Journal* (Washington, D.C.), February 6, 1982. Both articles cited rising congressional and executive branch concern about the lack of a reciprocal trading relationship with the other two countries.

16. Office of the U.S. Trade Representative, "Summary of Generalized System of Preferences Renewal Act of 1983," mimeo., Washington, D.C. (no date).

17. Christopher Madison, "Other Trade Issues Jeopardize Duty-free Program for Developing Nations," *National Journal,* February 18, 1984, Washington, D.C., p. 323.

18. Andrew James Samet and Gary Clyde Hufbauer, " 'Unfair' Trade Practices: A Mexican-American Drama," *Working Paper no. 1,* Overseas Development Council U.S.-Mexico Project, Washington, D.C., April 1982.

19. "Mexico to Enter Latin American Pact; Economic Union Appears Possible," *Mexico Update,* American Chamber of Commerce of Mexico, Mexico, D.F., October 15, 1986, p. 10.

20. Calls for greater cooperation along the U.S.-Mexican border include proposals for specific trade arrangements. See, for example, Congressman Richardson's proposals for a co-production zone between the United States and Mexico, reported in *Inside U.S. Trade,* Washington, D.C., October 24, 1986, pp. 13–14.

21. See the "Proposal for a Bilateral Commercial Agreement Between Mexico and the United States," Trade Subcommittee of the Binational Mexico-U.S. Business Committee, March 1985, p. 60.

4

Mexico's Entrance into the General Agreement on Tariffs and Trade

Alfredo Gutierrez Kirchner

Mexico has concluded the negotiations to become a member of the General Agreement on Tariffs and Trade (GATT). The Protocol of Accession was submitted to the GATT Contracting Parties during the last week of July 1986. It obtained approval of the full committee and the positive vote of forty-eight countries—among them the United States, the European Community, Brazil, Peru, Czechoslovakia, Poland, Cuba, and Nicaragua. Mexico obtained the two-thirds vote necessary to have the Protocol formally approved. In accordance with GATT provisions, the Protocol of Accession would become effective thirty days following Mexico's signature. Mexico's secretary of commerce and industrial development signed Mexico's adherence to the GATT *ad referendum* in August. After that, the Protocol required ratification by the Mexican Senate.

Mexico's negotiations to become a member of the GATT are contained in three documents: Mexico's Protocol of Accession to the General Agreement, the Report of the Working Group, and the List of Products negotiated by Mexico.

The Protocol of Accession

The Protocol of Accession is divided into several sections. The first is a "standard protocol" that corresponds to that used by most of the current members of the GATT. A foreword and certain operative sections cover Mexico's special interests. In this manner Mexico's accession to the GATT will be made on the basis of an ad hoc protocol.

The foreword addresses Mexico's condition as a developing country. In particular, Mexico will receive special and more favorable treatment as provided by the GATT and other instruments thereof. The foreword recognizes the priority granted by Mexico to its agricultural sector with regard to social and economic policies. It also discusses Mexico's program of gradual substitution for the previous import permit with a tariff protection, in a manner that is consistent with its objectives in this sector and in accordance with its commitment to eliminate import permits (as much as is possible).

The Protocol has established that the contracting parties are aware of Mexico's intentions to continue the implementation of its National Development Plan and its sectorial and regional programs, in accordance with the General Agreement. Mexico is committed to use trade policy instruments compatible with the GATT to maintain its regional and sectorial programs. The Protocol also addresses Mexico's energy resource programs. As indicated in paragraph five, "Mexico will exert its sovereignty over natural resources in accordance with the Political Constitution of the United Mexican States. Mexico will be able to maintain certain export restrictions relating to conservation of natural resources, in particular the energy sector, provided [that] such measures are taken in conjunction with restrictions on domestic production or consumption."

Mexico intends to maintain integrity and sovereignty over its energy sector. In mid-1986 the government announced a 10 percent cutback from its self-imposed crude oil export limit of 1.5 million barrels per day (bpd). As a result, PEMEX exports were reduced to 1.35 million bpd. Mexico does not view the program as inconsistent with GATT. Instead, inasmuch as the Protocol recognizes that decisions pertaining to Mexico's oil sector are a matter of sovereignty over natural resources mandated by the Mexican Political Constitution, this policy decision is within the parameters of the GATT. In an effort to curb domestic consumption, however, Mexico has increased the domestic prices of gasoline, fuel oil, and natural gas.

Report of the Working Group

The Report of the Working Group emphasizes many specific issues, including tariff policy, countervailing duties, and customs valuation. Article XX (g) of the GATT establishes that measures relating to conservation of exhaustible natural resources may be adopted. If such measures are effective in conjunction with restrictions on domestic production or consumption, these restrictions do not involve a one-to-one symmetrical cut. The obligations call for activity in the same direction with respect to both the external and the domestic sectors.

Mexico's commitment to a tariff policy is form. The country will bind its tariff to a maximum 50 percent duty for the whole Import Tariff Schedule. For the nine sectors covered by sectorial programs under the Pronafice, and within eight years from the date on which the Protocol becomes effective, duties higher than 50 percent may be used in such a way that up to half of a duty might be added to the normal tariff. The Mexican government has established that it intends to apply the 2.5 percent duty on the base value of the general import duty, and that the 3 and 10 percent additional duties provided for in Article 35 of the Customs Law as well as the 0.6 percent fee on the value of the merchandise to be imported will be charged in keeping with the previous import permits.

Mexico is committed to harmonize all customs valuation procedures with Article 7 of the General Agreement. Accordingly, the decision to eliminate official prices from the General Import Tariff Schedule no later than December 31, 1987, has been ratified.

Mexico's negotiations have addressed the issue of countervailing and antidumping duties. The safeguard clause of the Protocol reflects Mexico's position. Articles 14 and 15 of the Mexican Foreign Trade Law contain provisions granting the "injury test" for the application of countervailing duties to countries with which Mexico has signed an international agreement on subsidies and/or countervailing duties. The Foreign Trade Law also requires the injury test in the imposition of antidumping duties. Mexico has stated that it will implement safeguard measures in accordance with the General Agreement. In addition, the Mexican government has given its assurance that purchases by government-owned companies will be in accordance with Article 17, including notification and other procedures.

PEMEX and the GATT

PEMEX is no longer the sole importer of basic petrochemicals and lube oils. (At one time, it imported ten petrochemical products to supplement its production.) In late 1984 PEMEX instituted a new contractual system to buy these products. The imported petrochemicals and PEMEX's own production constituted the country's supply of basic petrochemicals. In 1984 PEMEX imported 870,000 tons of petrochemicals valued at $440 million. In 1985 these imports had increased to 1,200,000 tons at a value of $570 million.

Now that petrochemical and lube-oil users can import the products they once bought from PEMEX, the contractual suppliers of petrochemicals to PEMEX may look forward to dealing with an increased variety of Mexican clients. The Mexican government's new trade policy is such that PEMEX has advised former contractual suppliers that they may now sell directly to Mexican private customers; as a result, the PEMEX contracts were suspended.

Additional Trade Negotiations

Mexico held bilateral tariff discussions with ten countries as part of its negotiations to become a member of the GATT. These discussions resulted in concessions granted by Mexico on 373 tariff lines of the General Import Tariff Schedule, amounting to more than 15 percent of the total import value of 1985. Furthermore, Mexico negotiated a maximum duty of 50 percent. Mexico retained the power to establish additional duties—up to half the general import duty—in cases of exceptional importance, specifically in order to avoid the use of previous import permits. This rate may be applied until December 31, 1994.

Within the context of Mexico's decision to achieve structural change so as to recover domestic economic growth, Mexico may reach an "extended" agreement on trade and investment with the United States. This agreement would be negotiated under the GATT umbrella, and it would include sections on consultation, notification, and dispute settlement procedures.

A multilateral mechanism currently exercised by the Organization of American States covers consultation and notification procedures. As a concession to the differences in economic and social development within the region, the United States has agreed to consult the trade measures affecting the Latin American countries, but without requiring reciprocity. The mechanism that makes this action possible, created by Art. 170, is called the Special Committee for Consultation and Negotiation. Although this committee has not accomplished its original objective, it remains an alternative to the multilateral discussions of economic issues that affect the Inter-American system.

Mexico is committed to the GATT. Within six months of its accession, Mexico has stated that it will declare its intentions to become a signatory of the following codes: (1) import licensing, (2) customs valuation, (3) antidumping, and (4) technical obstacles. At the same time, Mexico will initiate negotiations in order to become a signatory of the Code on Subsidies and Countervailing Duties.

In 1985, in addition to Mexico's accession to the GATT, Mexico City and Washington signed the first bilateral agreement since the 1940s. But Mexico is overcoming a major crisis created by high public-sector deficits, trade imbalances, and hyperinflation. An important part of its program consists of bringing domestic prices more into line with international prices and keeping an exchange rate to avoid overvaluation of the currency. It is crucial that the fiscal deficit be reduced and positive trade balances be posted until the whole restructuring process takes place.

The government of President de la Madrid has invited the selective participation of foreign enterprises in the development of Mexico. A flexible application of the foreign investment law has accompanied this willingness, but such effort has to be supported by the policies of other governments. It is true that Mexico has to be particularly careful regarding investments in order to allow for the fact that during a period of serious crisis some policies have to be redefined, particularly when there is a need to save scarce foreign exchange. Nevertheless, Mexico has always been noted for its flexibility in implementing change with the least disturbance to existing interests.

The most important policy that the United States could adopt in order to support Mexico's recovery program would be to maintain an open market for the flow of Mexican exports. The revenue thus generated would have a twofold positive impact on the U.S. economy—namely, the indirect effect that U.S. suppliers would enjoy from increases in Mexican output due to the linkages between the two economies, and Mexico's ability to service its foreign debt through the revenue generated by added exports.

The United States must maintain an open market to Mexican exports. Although the current rate of exchange has promoted Mexican exports in the nonoil sectors to grow considerably, with the consequence that trade surpluses with the United States have been registered, the austerity program has continued to generate funds for the payment of the interest on the external debt, thus permitting the rescheduling of the principal. It would be a serious mistake to fail to take into consideration the relationship between trade and finance.

Trade relations between Mexico and the United States clearly benefit both; conversely, protectionist measures would defeat both of our economies as the economic borders closed. In short, let us continue to grow as trading partners with fair and reasonable accords to guide our economic relations.

PART THREE

The Implications of an Oil Economy: Benefits, Stakes, and "Petrodependency"

5

The Role of the Oil Industry in Mexico

Mario Ramón Beteta

Introduction: Oil and Sovereignty

Sovereignty is more than an abstract concept; it is exercised in our country, and petroleum is the tangible element of that exercise. In 1986, Mexico's president, Miguel de la Madrid Hurtado, maintained that economic adversity could be confronted by all of us through working harder, but not in exchange for sovereignty or the supreme course the Mexican people have traced for themselves. The oil community has taken up his words with special emotion and enthusiasm, because they reflect both the origin and the sense of our institution, Petróleos Mexicanos.

The petroleum industry has taken on not only economic importance but political importance as well. Mexico defines and defends itself by way of the Revolution—the true Revolution that translated itself, in a singularly faithful and exact manner, into the expropriation and founding of Petróleos Mexicanos, or PEMEX. Like the Revolution from which they came, the oil expropriation and PEMEX are a result of nationalistic drive, faith in ourselves, and the affirmation of our sovereignty.

In the light of these ideas, the Expropriation Decree of Lázaro Cárdenas acquires full and complete meaning. To dispose of our oil in an exclusive manner—as the sole and indisputable owner—was, is now, and will continue to be a sign and guarantee of independent life. In assuming direct dominion over hydrocarbons, the Mexican state not only rescued for its people this element of progress but confirmed categorically the role the constitution assigned to it as mentor and conductor of our economy. *Ours is a mixed economy, just as the constitution stipulates.* The government, as depositary of the people's will, oversees the great economic tasks, but it also sees to it that the spheres of public, private, and social initiative remain intact.

Mexico must reduce its dependence on oil. This is a fundamental objective of its long-term development strategy. The government is ready to stimulate the growth of exports and to improve their competitiveness. We will continue to rely on the exchange rate as a basic instrument for the promotion of exports. We need to increase nonoil exports and at the same time limit imports to bare essentials.

In the industrial countries many people resent the decrease in their exports to high-debt countries like Mexico, and they have also begun to feel the competition from Mexico's own exports. Shortsighted protective sentiments have hardened in many quarters, and in many instances, protective measures have been adopted. Witness, for instance, the U.S. actions against Mexican ammonia, gasoline, steel, glass, cement, and carbon black, to name but a few. Of course, world economic recovery and the expansion of world trade temper the temptation of protective barriers in the industrial countries. But growth itself is not enough; a better understanding of the problems of high-debt countries is needed as well.

PEMEX is the largest corporation in the developing world. It is a large-scale, diversified, highly integrated national oil company. Since 1938, PEMEX has had exclusive responsibility over all activities in the Mexican petroleum industry. Mexico has the fifth largest proven hydrocarbon reserves in the world. Among multinational oil corporations, only one produces more crude oil and natural gas liquids than PEMEX; likewise, only one U.S. corporation produces more natural gas.

Like other national oil corporations, PEMEX must pursue a wide set of corporate and social objectives. At the same time, it is subject to constraints not normally faced by privately owned oil companies. In addition to internal corporate goals such as profits and growth, PEMEX must respond to broader national economic policy objectives. The institutional complexity imposed by these multiple, and at times conflicting, demands constitutes a great managerial and political challenge.

The history of PEMEX adds to its complexity. Our institution is not among the recently formed national oil corporations: It was the first of its kind to be established. The circumstances under which PEMEX was created and its development over the past forty-six years make it more than just a company: It is a key political symbol of Mexican nationalism and economic independence.

PEMEX plays a strategic role in the country's current situation and prospects. Oil and gas exports account for 75 percent of Mexico's total merchandise exports, making PEMEX the main source of foreign exchange. In addition, PEMEX contributes directly with 36 percent of fiscal revenues, and almost a third of total public investment is directly carried out by the oil industry.

In 1982 Mexico was forced to ask for a deferral of principal payments on its foreign debt. This dramatic event shocked the financial world. It also reflected profound economic imbalances in Mexico. The economic crisis was the result of strategies and policies adopted in the 1970s, of deep structural disequilibria, and of a difficult international environment.

There is a clear relationship between the flag of the Insurgents of 1810, the flag of the revolutionaries of 1910 and 1917, and that of today's Mexico. In present-day Mexico, PEMEX safeguards one of the most precious of our natural resources, because, as we all know, it also lies at the heart of our independence.

PEMEX is and will continue to be one of the pillars of our economy and one of the major factors in our social cohesion and our development; however, Mexico is aware, and we share this conviction, that PEMEX is not, nor should it be, our sole support. We know, too, that the importance of what we are doing reflects the importance that petroleum has in today's world, but this neither signifies any special excellence on our part nor makes us worthy of any special privilege. Rather, it places on our shoulders many grave responsibilities and problems.

We are concerned about the welfare of our petroleum industry and about the efficient performance of the tasks we must complete. We are concerned about our contribution to energy independence, to economic independence, to the political independence of our country. However abundant or meager this contribution may be, it will always be imbued with our nationalist and revolutionary fervor. Oil is a product of our independence and our revolution, and PEMEX feels that its continuing urgent duty is to fight for these two fundamental causes, which are fully in force and must be defended. Complex economic problems weigh heavily on our nation's conscience. The difficulties Mexico confronts—many of them the result of mistakes and digressions of its own making—are derived also from the inequities of an egoistic system of international economies indifferent to the need for promoting the evolvement of developing countries.

To be authentic, this evolvement must be produced economically and socially in the sphere of sovereignty, which is an essential attribute of any state with its own roots and a genuine destiny. Such a process admits neither diminutions nor gradations; it is the basis but not the stuff of international negotiations. It is absolute or it is not sovereignty.

Our claim for a position in the forefront is not made out of pride or vanity. In the battle against the crisis, we ask only for the privilege of offering to form the vanguard of all our resources and all our energy and determination. PEMEX is immense; it has to be—in the worst of times and in the best. The difficulties of today do not intimidate us, just as they do not intimidate any Mexican. With hard work, efficiency, austerity, and honesty, we oil workers have joined forces to fight for the nation, and we assure you that our participation will not be limited. Before the entire nation, we reaffirm the decision to preserve for the country the sovereign ownership of what the petroleum industry is today and what it will be tomorrow—just as the political genius of Cárdenas conceived it yesterday.

Forget that the refining or manufacturing of basic petrochemicals may pass to foreign hands. Forget that only the most remote possibility exists for granting concessions to exploit our hydrocarbons. But let no one ever forget that, starting with Cárdenas—and, as Miguel de la Madrid Hurtado has vigorously ratified—Mexico's oil belongs to Mexico.

On March 18, 1938, Mexico City acclaimed the Oil Expropriation Decree with an enthusiasm and a faith before which no obstacle would prevail. There had been ominous forebodings on the horizon, but the citizenry were certain that these would be overcome, as assuredly they were. Other problems now weigh on our country, but the same faith and the same enthusiasm prevails. As a people we are intact. We are going to overcome every crisis we face just as we overcame the problems of the past.

Full dominion over oil wealth—which is the core of the country's historical patrimony—transformed its economic basis, making our political awareness both sharper and sounder. Once the aims of the oil expropriation took on constitutional standing, it became possible for Mexico to integrate all the phases of the industry—from exploration to distribution of the products derived from petroleum. With the industry thus integrated, the country is in absolute control of its internal energy picture, and it has sufficient strength to act with assurance in international circles.

The headquarters of the Worker's Confederation of Mexico is an illustrious entity in the battle for social rights, and one that was at the forefront during the memorable episodes of the oil expropriation. The Mexican petroleum industry salutes the Mexican labor movement, a sturdy pillar in our Revolution, and we render public acknowledgment to Fidel Velazquez—the man who, with passion and much experience, has headed this labor organization in defense of the people's causes. Here the decisive will of the workers strives to achieve its ideals, and vital energy is put behind the most transcendent battle of all—that which is fought for Mexico.

Mexico City is the nation's historical center and its future palace of generation. There for more than six centuries key events have been shaping our nationality. As a result of the tragic earthquake of September

1985, Mexico's capital city—deeply injured and pained—once more demonstrated the nobility of its sons and daughters and the courage with which it confronts adversity until such adversity is overcome. With its heart and mind the whole nation rallied around the city. No citizen was unaffected by this tragedy, and not a single one failed to help remedy it. Prominent among these were members of the oil community.

PEMEX is about to celebrate its fiftieth anniversary. In the interim, which compared to the magnitude of time that defines a nation's path is still brief, PEMEX has covered a great deal of ground. From the commercial isolation in which the expropriated companies tried to corner the institution, from the technological destitution in which it was left following the expropriation, from the first institutional vacillations, it has come to be one of the world's largest petroleum entities.

Its exploratory work never ceases. It pumps close to 3 million barrels of crude and over 3 billion cubic feet of gas daily; it has a refining capacity of over 1 million barrels daily; and its petrochemical facilities currently put out annually a little more than 12 million tons of a wide variety of products. PEMEX works 5,000 wells, and it operates 300 plants in 9 refineries and 17 petrochemical complexes. It has built 13,000 kilometers of roads and laid 50,000 kilometers of pipeline. It owns and operates the largest maritime fleet in the country, with 18 port installations and an extensive distribution and storage system.

Among all the world's industrial corporations—oil-related and otherwise—PEMEX occupies one of the top places in terms of earnings and sales. Among oil companies, it rates fourth in hydrocarbon production, fifth in reserves, and fifth also in exports. The institution, which in the midst of present uncertainties maintains its industrial potential, began without financial or technical support. What it did have was the support of the oil workers and the will and determination of our heroic people, who became one with Lázaro Cárdenas.

The initial moments of PEMEX and its subsequent trajectory constitute in themselves a lesson in valor and a test of capacity. They are proof of what we have been able to achieve and what we can do today in the face of new and serious difficulties. PEMEX is an exponent of the strength of Mexicans—a strength that multiplies itself when we rally round an idea.

Oil acts as a warp for the nation's economy; it is an element of capital importance. A gigantic enterprise, it represents for us enormous responsibilities. In oil, and in the parastatal organization in which Mexico safeguards and manages the oil, rests a substantial part of our development during the modern era. Our institution brings foreign exchange into the country; it strengthens public credit, reinforces our international personality, opens expectations, gives work to thousands of compatriots, and, above all, supplies the inhabitants of Mexico with more than 90 percent of their primary energy requirements.

What happens in the oil industry reverberates throughout the country. It is a huge echo chamber in which national events focus and multiply. Thus, it is not an island, nor could it be one; nor would the oil workers want it to be. Because if there is something we feel especially deeply, it is the commitment that links us to the community, without which neither our industry nor our Union would be anything.

Now when each step forward is laborious and arduous, the oil industry participates in what President de la Madrid has called "the battle for the nation." It gathers its forces and endeavors to strengthen its financial, operational, and administrative structures. The stronger the oil industry becomes, the better equipped it will be to contribute to the recovery of our economy.

Hydrocarbons have not lost their validity as capital resources. The fluctuations in the world oil market and the effects induced and unleashed deliberately for the monentary benefit of some countries and in detriment of others do not alter an essential truth—that this form of energy occupies a primary place in the contemporary world.

These years of decisive challenges and those that follow pose new demands and will require from all Mexicans a commitment and a discipline that we should begin cultivating with unswerving determination. The pace must be quickened and the process deepened in the evolutionary course of the industry's development. Circumstances call for it; moreover, our compatriots demand that efficiency and productivity be raised and that this be done with absolute honesty and devotion in the service of Mexico. Our confidence lies with the workers, technicians, and administrators of the institution to accomplish this.

Origins of the Crisis

Increases in international interest rates can have devastating effects on the external position of high-debt countries. On a yearly basis, to compensate every percentage point increase in the interest rate paid by Mexico, we would have to increase the level of Maya crude oil exports by 75,000 barrels per day or, alternatively, increase the average price of our crude oil exports by $1.30 per barrel.

Having successfully rescheduled all of its debt payments due between August 1982 and December 1984, Mexico has now negotiated a more ambitious financial package. Rescheduling will give payments due between 1985 and 1990 a more adequate maturity profile. The favorable evolution of Mexico's stabilization program and the clear political will to service all of our external obligations and to continue along the path set in our adjustment program have allowed our country to reach a basic understanding with the international financial community regarding rescheduling within a multiyear framework.

Oil exports have been a solid source of support for the balance of payments. In spite of the uncertainty that has prevailed in world oil markets, PEMEX has managed to maintain annual oil export revenues at $16 billion in 1982 and 1983. Our projected revenues for 1984 and 1985 are also in the $16 billion range.

The turnaround in the balance of payments in 1983 allowed the Central Bank to increase its foreign exchange reserves by $3.1 billion, given that it had started the year from a position in which monetary reserves were, for all practical purposes, nil. This reserve accumulation was possible owing to a 1983 trade surplus of almost $14 billion.

The 1983 trade surplus stemmed from, among other things, a 47 percent reduction in imports. During the first five months of 1984, however, Mexico generated a $6.4 billion trade surplus in spite of a 30 percent increase in imports. This surplus, of course, is symptomatic of economic recovery. At the same time, nonoil exports increased by a little less than 50 percent. Today, Central Bank reserves amount to $6.9 billion.

The short-term economic and social costs of Mexico's financial crisis and adjustment process cannot be underestimated. In 1982 gross domestic product decreased by one-half of 1 percent, and in 1983 economic activity contracted by almost 5 percent. There is no precedent in modern Mexican history for such a deep recession.

The control of inflation is a key prerequisite of long-term stable growth. The struggle against inflation is a daily one, and, given its momentum, there are no easy or rapid solutions. In 1982 the increase in the consumer price index reached a record level of almost 100 percent. Although we are still far from taming the inflationary beast, significant advances have been made. Inflation during the first half of 1984 was lower than that during the same period in 1983, and monthly inflation rates have been systematically decreasing.

In 1985, we celebrated three anniversaries—the forty-seventh anniversary of the petroleum expropriation, the one hundred and seventy-fifth anniversary of Miguel Hidalgo's launch of the War of Independence with his call to arms in Dolores, and the seventy-fifth anniversary of the revolutionary spark kindled by Aquilles Serdan in the capital of the state of Puebla. It was in the state of Puebla that our Revolution caught fire. We are reminded of how Mexico solved its grave problems in other epochs, of how it has reached its goals one by one, and of how it is solving its problems today thanks to the faith, enthusiasm, solidarity, and fundamental nationalism of its people.

To recall the movements of 1810 and 1910 is to enhance our identity, our dignity, and our sovereignty. But remembrance is not enough. We must continue to act in accordance with the guidelines laid down by the Mexican people and their leaders in those highly critical times, and we must meditate not only on the events themselves but also on the meaning of these events. There is a straight line connecting the struggle for independence and the revolutionary epic. The people of Hidalgo and Morelos, as well as those of Madero and Carranza, successfully pursued the same ideals. The oil expropriation confirmed and implemented, in one of the key areas of our economy, the principles that had been postulated since these times.

When Lázaro Cárdenas issued the expropriation decree, he was echoing the beliefs associated with both our independence and our revolution. The will of our country had become stronger and clearer, and on March 18, 1938, it reached its irreversible climax with regard to our great national wealth—petroleum. Through Lázaro Cárdenas, Mexico advanced its efforts toward economic independence and took its rightful place as a sovereign country whose dignity, based on reason and law, is beyond the reach of the ambitions of the powerful.

Prospects for the Future

Exploration for hydrocarbons is the first link in a long chain of activities that culminate in the delivery of the processed products to the consumer. Between ten and fifteen years elapse from the beginning of exploration work until economically profitable production is obtained. The petroleum industry is a long-term activity and therefore requires careful planning. In 1984, for example, 1,200 "group-months" were devoted to exploratory studies in the field, and 85 teams were assigned to exploratory drilling that yielded 59 wells, of which 14 turned out to be producers. These activities resulted in the discovery of ten oil fields— three off-shore and seven on land.

PEMEX has earmarked an unprecedented volume of resources for exploratory activity, which will be increased even further in the coming years, in order to recover and, if possible, surpass the former level of our reserves. Nevertheless, the reader should bear in mind that there is not always a direct relationship between the resources used for exploration and the results obtained.

The annual extraction levels that were reached between 1982 and 1985—on the order of 1.3 billion barrels of liquid hydrocarbons—made Mexico the fourth largest world producer of crude oil. Given the volumes extracted, huge investments must now be made in order to meet the objective of at least maintaining reserves at their present level of about 72 billion barrels. Each year, we must discover and test drill the equivalent of more than two entire fields of those classified as giant (deposits of this size are only infrequently discovered worldwide).

Thanks to exploratory work, proven hydrocarbon reserves continue to be adequate. On December 31, 1984, proven reserves were estimated at more than 71 billion barrels of liquid hydrocarbon, only slightly lower than the total for 1983. Although a decline of 1 percent is no cause for concern, it does suggest that we should reflect on the future.

Hydrocarbons are nonrenewable resources and are therefore finite. For this reason, and given that the period of cheap and abundant energy is coming to an end, we must be increasingly conscious of how important it is for the country to save hydrocarbons and to use them economically and rationally. As we make progress in using and conserving our energy resources, we shall be able to prolong our export capacity and, with it, our foreign exchange earnings. Above all, we shall be able to maintain our current level of self-sufficiency.

In 1984, 2.7 million barrels of crude oil were produced daily—a quantity .7 percent greater than the total for 1983; 65 percent of this amount came from the offshore area of Campeche. Gas production was 3.75 billion cubic feet a day, or 7.4 percent less than in 1983. The installation of the equipment and the additives required for making full use of the associated gas in plants offshore and on land made it possible to recover the condensates that previously had to be flared. Moreover, 228 development wells were drilled in 1983, with an 83 percent success rate of 190 producers. The sole purpose of most of these wells is to maintain production at current levels.

There is always a significant natural decline in oil deposits that must be counteracted by drilling new wells. In some cases, the natural decline is offset by a secondary recovery system. In 1984, under this system, 775,000 barrels of water were injected daily in order to maintain pressure in certain oil fields. For the same purpose, an enormous complex is currently being developed to inject 1.5 million barrels a day into the Gulf of Campeche Abkatun oil field.

PEMEX has nine refineries, which include 150 processing plants and their corresponding auxiliary services. These installations transform crude oil, gas, and liquid condensates into the fuels needed by the country. In accordance with foreseeable needs, work is under way on new constructions and expansions. In 1984, expansion of the Poza Rica and Salamanca refineries was completed, and the second stages of the Tula and Salina Cruz refineries, still under construction, are expected to begin operation in 1987 and 1989 respectively.

The Future Growth of Oil Exploration and Development

Knowledge of the country's hydrocarbon reserve is fundamental to the petroleum industry. According to the calculations of our technicians, certified by the Mexican Petroleum Institute, Mexico's total proven hydrocarbon reserves stood at more than 70 billion barrels as of December 31, 1985. This figure confirms the number of wells we have drilled, two of which reached record-breaking depths in Latin America of over 7,000 meters.

Exploratory activity at PEMEX is, and will continue to be, intense. In 1985, 112 brigades of geologists and geophysicists carried out various studies, while another 107 interpreted and evaluated the information gathered in the field. Locations were fixed and proposals were made to drill deep wells so as to confirm the existence of the expected oil fields. These will doubtless be our production wells at the start of the twenty-first century.

The 92 rigs used for exploration drilled through a total of 318 kilometers of rock during 1985; 69 exploratory wells were completed, and 19 of these represented either oil discoveries in new structures or confirmations of the existence of oil in neighboring fields already in production. With these discoveries, exploratory efforts started some years back were concluded.

Using 108 rigs, 219 development wells were drilled at depths fluctuating between 1,800 and 6,500 meters. Upon confirmation of our knowledge of these areas, 81 percent proved to be production wells of hydrocarbons—a figure higher than the international average. These development wells make it possible to incorporate new volumes into domestic output, thus offsetting the natural declines in the producing oil fields.

To support extraction, 108 pulling units have been used in addition to other techniques, such as water injection, to maintain the energy of the oil fields themselves. These procedures resulted in an average of 2,630,000 barrels per day (bpd) of crude pumped during the past year. Average output over the last three years was 2,660,000 bpd.

Production of natural gas during the year stood at 360 million cubic feet per day (cfd). Of this amount, 84 percent was associated with crude flows, while the rest was obtained from fields exclusively producing gas.

The Advantages and Vulnerabilities of a World Oil Market

The instability shown by the world oil market during the past years became more acute in 1985 and 1986. In June 1986, only 783,000 bpd were exported, and the first half of 1985 closed with an average of 1.337 million bpd. With the establishment of differential prices, it was possible, however, for the various parts of the world in which Mexican crude is traded to recover volume during the second half of the year. Thus, the annual export average reached 1.483 million bpd in 1985—only 4 percent below the programmed 1.5 million bpd.

Foreign exchange income for crude sales during 1985 was $13.296 billion—down by $1.670 billion from 1984. This drop was as much the result of lower export volume as of the average price level, which was almost $1.50 less than the previous year's level.

In 1985 domestic demand for refined products—gasoline, diesel fuel, and others—was up 3 percent over 1984 levels to 1.140 million bpd. Total output exceeded demand, and the surplus was placed in foreign markets. The average of 145,000 bpd exported added up to an additional foreign exchange income of $1.233 billion—up 21 percent over the previous year.

To cover shortages that occurred in some products and to ease problems of distribution to certain regions of the Republic, liquefied gas and fuel oil were imported. The trade balance in this respect, however, favored PEMEX by more than $750 million dollars—a direct result of higher efficiency levels in our refineries, brought about chiefly through better maintenance.

On the other hand, a better utilization of liquids and condensates over the last three years has led to a substantial increase in the production of liquefied gas. Yet we have not been able to keep up with domestic demand, which has been distorted by the use of this energy as fuel in motor-driven vehicles.

Industrial Diversification and Petrochemicals

Basic petrochemicals, a relatively new activity for PEMEX, have shown extraordinary dynamism, supplying the country with the products required by the secondary petrochemical industry. Nonetheless, Mexico must import some basic petrochemicals in order to satisfy internal demand, which amounted to less than 8 percent of our production but more than $500 million dollars in 1984 alone. In short, we have the capacity to satisfy our needs in the majority of products, with margins for export in some.

Although La Congrejera—Latin America's largest petrochemical complex—is in full opration, and the output of basic petrochemicals totaled more than 1 million tons monthly duirng 1985, production has not been sufficient to avoid deficits in certain areas. The oil industry has been making considerable investments in the petrochemicals sector, but limitations in resources have forced us to give preference to products with higher priority in the country's industry. The trade balance in basic petrochemicals for 1985 showed a negative balance of $485 million dollars, owing to the imports made to meet the demand for secondary petrochemical products.

Another aspect of the petrochemicals sector is the treatment of gas emerging from the wells in association with crude oil and the liquids and condensates that accompany it. Among those liquids are propane and butane (commonly known as liquefied gas), which in Mexico are used mainly as domestic fuel and are thus especially valuable. Their production is limited by that of natural gas, which in turn is limited by the volume of crude that is extracted. Therefore, the available volume of liquefied gas cannot be independently increased. The need to restrict its use arises not from lack of productive capacity on the part of PEMEX nor from scarcity of natural resources, but from the rational principles that govern our exploitation and use of hydrocarbons.

During 1984, for example, various units for treating gas and liquids were put into operation in the Nuevo PEMEX Petrochemical Complex, which President de la Madrid inaugurated in 1983. The installation of the Petrochemical Complexes of Ciudad PEMEX and Cactua were also improved, and when these were integrated with Nuevo PEMEX, greater flexibility and reliability in the system was obtained. These developments have permitted the establishment of bases for better use of these products.

Domestic Trade and the Mexican Economy

One of the fundamental tasks of PEMEX is to guarantee the domestic supply of basic petroleum and petrochemical products. The transport and distribution of hydrocarbons is accomplished with greater efficiency due to the availability of an improved infrastructure—ports, pipelines, storage tanks, and terminals—as well as new planning and operational control mechanisms. The solidarity and coordinated action of the workers, officials, distributors, consumers, and the authorities allow the continuing supply of liquefied gas to the population of the Valley of Mexico without great inconvenience. We are now actively engaged in a general redesign of the distribution system for distillates and liquefied gas in the Valley of Mexico. We have also made progress in the engineering of a new supply system whose central pivot will be the Tula terminal in the state of Hidalgo. Sales of petroleum products increased at an annual rate of 6 percent and those of petrochemicals at 16 percent.

Overall growth in the demand for petrochemical products was linked to a marked alteration in their consumption structure. The rapid increase in demand for liquefied gas has compelled us to import growing amounts of the fuel, and the relevant authorities have adopted various restrictive measures, among them higher prices for nondomestic use. Yet considerable progress has been made in modernizing the price structure of petroleum and petrochemical products. The pricing policy, established by the federal government, and to which PEMEX contributes within its scope, has not only been an efficient instrument for increasing tax revenues but has also encouraged a more rational use of energy. A clear example of the latter is the moderation now witnessed in the use of gaoline, diesel fuel, and natural gas. In short, we have been able to adjust the structure of fuel demand to its availability and relative cost.

Curiously, in 1984 total consumption of hydrocarbons grew at the same rate as the gross national product, in contrast to the experience of the 1970s, when consumption grew at a much higher rate than that of economic activity as a whole. This return to reason has contributed to the structural changes postulated by Mexico's economic development policy with regard to energy savings and conservation.

The Implications of International Trade

Mexico's petroleum policy has contributed to the stability of the international petroleum market and to the continuity of the inflow of foreign currency that the country receives as a result of our petroleum exports. The efforts made to bring greater order and balance to the international market have meant intense activity on Mexico's part in many forums; indeed, Mexico has had to approach numerous organizations and governments of producing and consuming countries. Our trade practice has been exemplary in its clarity. Mexico has sold all its crude under long-term contracts with established clients. All PEMEX's transactions have been carried out at official prices. We have not speculated by selling crude on the spot market, nor have we taken part in barter operations.

For example, during 1984 PEMEX exported crude petroleum, petroleum products, natural gas, and basic petroleum products totaling $1.66 billion, which represented 69 percent of the country's total exports of goods. Sales were made to 45 clients in 22 countries. The United States acquired 49 percent of total shipments, and Spain and Japan followed the United States on the list of major purchasers of Mexican petroleum.

Import substitution has taken on special significance inasmuch as it gives strong impetus to the country's industry and helps decrease commercial and technological dependence on foreign suppliers. The Import Substitution Committee and fourteen subcommittees of PEMEX maintain ongoing relationships with Mexican firms; accordingly, they are informed of future requirements so that they can undertake new lines of manufacturing with assurance. For the first time, Mexican firms have been advised of our estimated needs for the next five years. In addition, they are offered technical advice through the Mexican Petroleum

Institute and are helped to obtain credit from the Mexican banking institutions. Without PEMEX, large portions of the country would have a totally different existence than the one that they have today; they would be free of some of the problems that PEMEX causes, but they would also lack many of the opportunities that PEMEX provides. In particular, the construction of roads, bridges, and health and education centers in the areas surrounding PEMEX's work sites have benefited both its own personnel and the local communities.

The Economies of Oil

The economic and financial success of the oil industry has been a result of stricter measures taken in operations and investments, better control of its budgets, increased productivity, and reduced costs. The positive difference between revenue and spending—that is, the operational surplus—was close to $17.6 billion in 1985. This made it possible for PEMEX to make a fiscal contribution of $13.3 billion—$8.8 billion in corporate taxes and almost $4.4 billion in withholding taxes. These payments represented half of the fiscal income of the federal government and 55 percent of PEMEX revenue.

The earnings generated since 1982 have made it possible to multiply by nineteen times the equity reserves accumulated up to that year. At the same time, the value of our total assets quadrupled. More than half of these assets are currently financed with company capital, whereas in 1982 the proportion was one-fourth. The debt of PEMEX dropped from $19.8 billion to $15.7 billion—a reduction of one-fifth over the three-year period.

Total foreign exchange revenue in 1985 was $15,115,000,000—down 9 percent from 1984 levels. This reduction of income from abroad was offset by reduced spending in dollars. PEMEX used only 12 percent of total foreign exchange revenue to cover expenditures in operations and investments, and 18 percent for servicing its debt. The remaining 70 percent was made available to the country for other economic activities.

The management of the nation's oil industry considers individuals to be its greatest asset. At all our work centers, there are men and women whose work—whether manual or highly technical, risky or not, managerial, scientific, or administrative, in the field, on the sea, in refineries or at petrochemical plants, in hospitals or at schools, behind a desk or on a drilling platform—is of great value. The mental, moral, and physical energy utilized by all have built and given impetus to Mexico's oil industry. The permanent concern of the institution for its workers has become a reality in the form of training programs in which close to a third of the personnel benefit each year from 400,000 hours of instruction; in the form of housing programs that, in the past four years, have provided more than 11,000 new homes; and in the form of high-quality medical assistance and prevention programs, which during 1985 protected more than a million beneficiaries.

The function of industrial safety has never been exercised with such intensity at PEMEX as in recent years. On-the-job, personal-accident frequency indexes have been reduced by 23 percent over the past three years, and serious-injury indexes are now 35 percent lower than in 1982. Better on-the-job safety levels have much to do with increased maintenance, which has been given the priority it deserves. The Special Bipartisan Commission established by instructions from President de la Madrid and made up of members from management and labor has contributed to increased safety levels. These members have visited the majority of PEMEX work centers to verify the conditions under which workeres operate and have resolved many of the problems brought to their attention while referring other issues to the correct authorities.

The National Ecology Commission, headed by President de la Madrid, recently undertook a series of initiatives to improve the quality of the air in the Valley of Mexico—an area to which our institution is highly committed. PEMEX's main responsibility consists of substituting fuels and improving the quality of those fuels distributed. Emissions of sulphur dioxide, lead, carbon monoxide, unburned hydrocarbons, and other pollutants will be lowered even further this year. The institution has been able to respond rapidly to these needs, primarily because of the studies and programs on the matter that have been in progress for years. In addition, the Department of the Federal District (DDF), the Federal Electricity Commission (CFE), and PEMEX have agreed to make geophysic and echo-sounding studies in the valley of Mexico. Their aim is to establish a basis for a new building code in benefit of the metropolitan zone.

PEMEX has continued granting support to domestic industry through its import-substitution program by using Mexican goods and services in ever-larger proportions. Since 1982, we have placed more than 2 million orders covering purchases for more than 1 billion pesos. In 1981, two-thirds of our acquisitions were imported; in 1985, imports represented only one-sixth of our purchases. In other words, in 1985, for each peso spent on purchases from abroad, five went into domestic industry.

During the first three years of President de la Madrid's administration, the management of PEMEX—with the effective support of the workers—resolved to stress efficiency, transparency, and the spirit of service. Historically, the institution has complied with such tasks. Nonetheless, it was neccessary to ensure that the programs and plans were being executed with increasingly strict adherence to rigid standards and that they were being methodically and punctually followed up. Although considerable advances have been made, we must continue our movement toward the goals of increased efficiency, honesty, and service to the community.

The administration of PEMEX is clearly aware of the upsets suffered by the economy as a whole—upsets that the administration is confronting with strict austerity policies. These upsets, however, annul neither public liberties nor the exercise of democracy, nor the vigor of our political institutions, nor acts that are oriented toward the benefit of majorities. The collapse of international oil prices—the result of a fundamental imbalance between the potential supply and the real demand of crude in the world—constitutes a problem that for Mexico, as for other oil-exporting countries, requires a rapid solution.

In barely three months, world prices of the principal crudes were reduced by half. Mexican oil was no exception. The price of Isthmus crude fell from $27 per barrel in November 1985 to $13 by mid-March 1986. During the same period, Maya crude dropped eleven dollars, recently reaching a level of close to $12 per barrel. The international price is now similar in real terms to what it had been in 1974. It is obvious that this reduction in oil prices has serious implications for the Mexican economy, particularly with regard to the dependence of our country's balance of payments and public finances upon oil revenue.

The substantial fluctuations in international oil prices have forced us to avail ourselves of the flexibility of our institution. In July 1985, PEMEX established price differentials according to the geographical location of clients, which made possible the recovery of sales that in months before had been cut sharply. In December 1985, when the situation was becoming increasingly turbulent, it was necessary to set into motion a system whereby prices were fixed each month in retrospective. In early 1986, we again began negotiating with our clients the automatic price mechanism, which tends to link the price of our crudes with other widely marketed brands.

We continue to seek stability in this area, and we abstain from participating in irregular commercial practices. No discounts are offered, nor are we involved in speculative maneuvers. All of these efforts have contributed to our prestige as serious, responsible, and thoroughly trustworthy suppliers, which is no small accomplishment in these times.

Our priority is to reach an agreement among exporters on rationalizing production. With this specific aim and with others related to the problem, Mexico is prepared to proceed in its dialogue with various countries, and to participate in negotiations that are oriented toward reordering the international supply of hydrocarbons. We have advocated and continue to advocate the design of an effective mechanism to this end— one that will serve both exporting and consumer nations.

From PEMEX's standpoint, the world crude market is a matter of efficiency and productivity as well as a cause for comment and preoccupation in wide sectors of the public. Regarding the question of the cost of production, I categorically declare that such cost favors us when compared to that of the most prosperous oil enterprises. Mexican oil deposits—particularly those that are relatively young in the region of Chiapas-Tabasco and offshore from Campeche—are as generous as any in the world.

On the other hand, and as we have stated on numerous occasions before the entire country, PEMEX has a technology comparable to the most advanced in the world. Our technological know-how has been accumulating over the years and has lately been a decisive factor in pushing up productivity levels, with the resulting reduction of costs.

Despite the foregoing, however, the economic significance and strategic importance of hydrocarbons compel us to study the world situation day by day and to examine each of its implications. Our participation in export markets will depend not only on cost per barrel and its relation to prevailing prices but also on deeper reasons, prominent among which is the need to safeguard the national interest. In short, Mexico will not undersell its petroleum.

While observing as carefully as possible the prevailing standards and paying special attention to maintenance costs, which will not be affected, we will have to reduce current spending and make painful adjustment measures. Regarding investments, we will be left in the position of deciding which activities must continue and which will need to be postponed. Economic restriction will also force us to focus exploration and development activity on the most promising regions and deposits, in order to obtain maximum yield with fewer resources.

Notwithstanding the tight situation in which we must operate in the immediate future, in dealing with third parties PEMEX will observe the order and seriousness on which we have insisted so much. We will proceed with our import-substitution policy as a basic support element to Mexico's industrial plant, and we will continue to give ample backing to the suppliers of goods and services from whom we have received signs of cooperation. In addition, we will orient the domestic production of basic petrochemicals toward those products that, through the secondary petrochemical industry and manufacturers, provide the greatest added value within the country.

Internal prices of PEMEX products will continue to be fixed by the Public Sector Commission on Rates and Prices and to be linked to the aims of the country's economic policies. Prices will also undoubtedly tend to support public finances, to encourage the progress of the institution, and to avoid the wasteful or inconvenient use of hydrocarbons.

Moreover, the systems of transport and distribution used by PEMEX will continue to be modernized so that costs can be cut down and safety increased. Among the necessary structural changes in the economy will be the revision of the systems and policies involved in this process of modernization.

In the area of maritime transport, we want to ratify the policy of the de la Madrid administration toward Mexicanization of the fleet at the service of PEMEX and elimination of intermediaries in this activity. We have incorporated two large tankers into our major fleet and ordered the construction of four more. At the same time, we have added various units to our minor fleet. We will continue the process of Mexicanization, but, given the scarcity of resources we face at PEMEX, the private sector in Mexico will have to take on a larger share of the process.

Because of the problems afflicting us at this time, we will have to apply our intelligence and make sacrifices as never before in order to defend what is ours. At PEMEX, this stance will be our banner. The Revolutionary Union of Oil Workers of the Mexican Republic, and management—both of which have long proven their nationalism—propose to continue to work unceasingly and in accord in order to overcome the difficult situation facing us.

The matter is one of unity and solidarity, of working together. At PEMEX, only workers exist—Mexican workers, unionized or not, working in a managerial, technical, skilled, or unskilled capacity. We are all workers, and our efforts are made for the nation; and PEMEX belongs in its entirety to the nation and its people.

We are confronted by a whole series of obstacles, which we can neither deny nor diminish. We are in a difficult situation, and the only legitimate attitude for dealing with it is a combative one. I speak of a sensible and reasonable combativeness—one that will allow us to exercise the full potential of our institution in the most useful way for the country, in a way that will not entail hastiness or retreat.

PEMEX is Mexico's largest and most solid enterprise. It has been an engine of major progress and now must be resistant in the face of adversity. In either of these roles, it remains faithful to its essential mission, which consists of endeavoring to bring about, through the intelligent and patriotic use of hydrocarbons, the greatest good for the country of Mexico.

With both clarity and precision, President de la Madrid has alerted us to the stumbling blocks in the nation's economy. The petroleum industry realizes the magnitude and the seriousness of the situation, and we are resolved to accept the sacrifices required of us. We are convinced that Mexico will emerge from these difficult times a strengthened nation. This matter concerns us all, as countrymen, without exception. But PEMEX, as an institution of the Republic and as an organization industry, belongs—as ever—to Mexico.

6

Mexico: Petroleum Stakes and Risks in a Turbulent Marketplace

Edward L. Morse

Petroleum, Mexico's largest export, generates two-thirds of governmental receipts of foreign exchange and one-third of the government's budget. It is also the most important commodity by which Mexico can seek to maximize export earnings and export values. As a durable commodity, oil is the main resource upon which Mexico can leverage its financial rebound. Value maximization and financial leverage are the primary instruments through which Mexico can ensure reasonable economic growth and a gradual reduction in the indebtedness of the country.

Mexico should follow a strategy of value maximization for several reasons. For one thing, as I have just pointed out, oil is Mexico's most important product. The value Mexico receives for oil should be primary among the competing goals its seeks to pursue in the short term. Take, for example, the competing claim of the OPEC countries—Saudi Arabia in particular, perhaps—that Mexico, like the other non-OPEC oil exporters, should refrain from increasing its export volumes in the current market to avoid upsetting OPEC's delicate pricing strategy. Should Mexico substantially increase its crude oil export volumes, many argue, there would be a direct impact on the world oil market. According to this line of argument, not only would Mexico upset the pricing balance OPEC has sought to secure, but in the long run the value received from Mexican oil exports would be reduced.

Mexico has chosen a strategy of cooperation with OPEC. Though not an official member of OPEC, Mexico has participated at some recent OPEC meetings and has pledged cooperation in limiting export volumes. Many Mexicans feel that full membership would deprive Mexico both of autonomy and of "bargaining leverage," and that its current posture facilitates a courting by OPEC, perhaps promising Mexico a greater "allowance" for exports once world demand increases. But this argument is faulty on several counts. Since January 1981, oil exports from the United Kingdom and Norway have increased by about 500,000 barrels per day. Despite sometimes acerbic criticism from OPEC members, the U.K. in particular has refused to limit its production. British and Norwegian officials also maintain an open dialogue with key OPEC countries on their oil production policies. As with the North Sea countries, there is no reason why Mexico could not walk this diplomatic tightrope with incremental increases in production and export levels. Mexico's current OPEC strategy of "independent concession," however, seems to provide neither the advantages of membership nor those of true independence. Instead, its strategy of cooperation with OPEC is risky and does not guarantee anything for Mexico. Why would OPEC grant privileges to Mexico at the expense of a member? On the other hand, why should Mexico grant the Saudis or any other OPEC member a say in their most important policy decision?

Thus we come to the second reason for which Mexico should pursue a value maximization strategy. If the pricing structure of OPEC is upset, it will be for reasons outside of Mexico's control, not by any action Mexico might take. No matter what Mexico's policies might have been in the winter of 1985-1986, for example, Mexico could not have prevented the free fall in the price of oil by more than 50 percent. Any future price reduction or increase that might take place will have little to do with Mexican exports.

A third reason has to do with additional opportunity costs. Current oil markets are extremely turbulent and are likely to remain so for another three to five years. Supply pressures in the marketplace stem from persistent weakness in demand and from the desire of individual producer countries to increase their production levels at the margin. The Mexican government risks temporary and long-term losses that might never be recouped if it does not maximize the value it receives for exports by increasing volumes.

Today's supply pressures are bound to increase once the Iran-Iraq war winds down. The resolution of that conflict—surely within the next five years—will mean substantially increased pressure on prices as increased productive capacity from both Iran and Iraq is gradually restored.

Mexico can choose to continue the conservative "follow-the-leader" strategy it has been pursuing since 1981. That strategy, however, would result in little more than kowtowing to OPEC on prices, credit terms, and production and export levels. The further result, almost inevitably, would be additionally reduced values for Mexico's exports and further erosion in export earnings. Mexico's alternative would be to maintain its tradition of autonomy and independence in the oil market as in other areas of international trade, and to forge a bold and forceful "Mexico-first" strategy. Such a strategy would maximize the value Mexico receives for its most precious natural resource.

A first category of efforts can be described as short-term revenue maximization, a process that includes both direct revenue maximization and preventive action. With respect to revenue maximization, the most obvious step the Mexican government can take is to facilitate an increase in production and exports—a desirable outcome not only in terms of short-term gains but also with respect to the longer term. Inasmuch as petroleum prices will continue to slide, regardless of Mexico's oil policy, Mexico would do well to follow the example of the North Sea countries by producing incrementally as much crude as it can and as much as the market will bear.

PEMEX may well be finding it difficult to increase production because of both the erosion of surplus production capacity and the capital costs involved in creating a surplus capacity for a depletable resource such as oil. Mexico has for all practical purposes terminated capital investments in new exploration and production projects. Expansion of these investments is critical if Mexico is to have the export capacity needed to service its debts five to ten years from now. In fact, it would be a prudent policy for Mexico's creditors to insist on a tie-in between loan restructuring and new capital investments in petroleum. In any event, the capital budgeting burden would be eased substantially through enhanced production.

One potential objection to increasing production in the short term is that additional crude for exports is most likely to filter into the U.S. market—and successive Mexican governments have not wanted to become overly dependent upon this market. It is time for Mexico to review its marketing strategy, based on a value maximization approach. Mexico must determine precisely which crude market actually provides the best potential return. This can be done only on a netback basis, an approach Mexico has thus far eschewed for poor reasons. In particular, it has argued that netback pricing deprives Mexico of pricing autonomy. But it is an illusion to believe that in today's market buyers will have any other perspective for their oil-purchasing strategies.

Revenue maximization involves more than direct measures. It also encompasses a range of preventive measures that might be pursued more diligently than in the past. First, PEMEX could go much further than before by creating auditable production and revenue accounting procedures and processes. Although it is difficult to specify the savings that could be generated by auditable accounting practices, it is clear in the oil industry that leakage from Mexico's production and revenue still occurs. This leakage could be greatly minimized, however, through modernization of the means by which PEMEX develops its data such that the data would become more transparent and reliable than is currently the case. Here, too, creditors should be more vigilant than they have been and insist that, as a part of loan rescheduling, Mexico install accounting procedures that conform to standards set in the industry.

In terms of prevention, Mexico can also begin actively to hedge against future price surprises—specifically by trading paper barrels on the futures market. There are indications that Mexico has, in fact, begun this process. Such a step would be inexpensive; it could also be regarded as an insurance policy against price surprises. In addition, by trading on a futures basis, PEMEX could obtain a minimum future income stream from oil sales, thereby creating a much more reliable planning baseline of income and expenditure.

Longer-term mechanisms for revenue maximization should also be considered. We can assume that over the long run, Mexico, like other oil producers, will want to integrate downstream in order to gain added value in an eventually tighter marketplace and to enhance overall marketing flexibility. We can also assume that Mexico may confront political uncertainty with respect to legislation impeding product imports in the United States. By the same token, we can conclude that it would be prudent for Mexico to look into opportunities to obtain downstream facilities in the country's major marketplace. Both the option to buy refineries and the negotiation of actual equity stakes in exchange for processing would have been very inexpensive to Mexico in 1983–1985. Today, the costs of downstream integration have increased, but they are certainly still justified given the rebound in downstream profitability. PEMEX should therefore look aggressively into the possibilities of making such deals in the near future.

In addition to taking steps to maximize revenue, Mexico should consider the mechanisms necessary to gain financial leverage from its crude resources. Such leverage is particularly important in the current and prospective economic climate for Mexico. Mexico has actually had a tradition of innovation in the use of petroleum as a financial instrument. Oil-linked bonds were issued by Mexico in 1977. They were misused by Mexico when it decided to convert pesos into dollars at an overvalued exchange rate. Mexico also experimented with this form of financing in the $1 billion pre-export payment of crude for the Strategic Petroleum Reserve (SPR) by the U.S. government in 1982. That arrangement was praised as an innovative step enabling Mexico to secure hard currency at a time when Mexico's debt-servicing situation was particularly precarious. However, it has also been criticized for short-changing Mexico on the grounds that the oil was discounted too deeply. Still, there is no reason why further innovations should be dismissed. Mexico can build on its experience in this area and develop financial mechanisms to leverage its borrowings on terms much improved over those achieved in 1977 or 1982. The goal would be the same: injection of additional hard currency more rapidly into the Mexican economy at lower interest rates.

A related approach would be the establishment of a floating storage system for crude oil close to Mexico's major markets. Given the distressed price of tankerage in recent years, it might make sense for Mexico to create such a system, for two reasons. First, it would provide Mexico greater flexibility in marketing crude. In the past, when Mexico could not make price adjustments rapidly enough, it lost market share and was unable to recoup it. Floating storage would provide a buffer against this problem. Second, it would enable Mexico to build another basis for collateralized borrowing. If, for borrowing purposes, either crude or product were placed on the high seas in a floating storage system, any loan thereby generated could also be substantially, if not fully, hedged by trading such oil forward.

The steps outlined above are obviously debatable. Equally obvious, they are not as simple to implement in practice as they might be in theory. For that matter, there may be legitimate reasons not to proceed on some of them. However, these lines of action do suggest that with innovative thinking and autonomous action, both of which are well within Mexico's tradition, much can be done through the use of Mexico's most precious resource to enhance the country's trade balance and its ability to manage its debt.

7

The International Economic Crisis and the Battle for the Nation

René Villarreal

Translated by Edith Grossman

The deepening international oil crisis as of 1986 clarified once again the fact that the fundamental structural problem in the Mexican economy lies in foreign vulnerability: For each dollar that the price of oil goes down, more than $500 million annually are not collected; a 1 percent increase in international interest rates means payments of more than 700 million additional dollars in debt service, and a 1 percent decrease in the growth rate of the industrialized nations (or an equivalent drop in their external demand because of neoprotectionist measures) increases by $500 million the deficit in Mexico's current balance of payments.

In other words, the impact of the crisis that the world economy is experiencing in the areas of oil, finance, and trade has made the Mexican economy more vulnerable in this decade than at any other time in recent history. In the past, the increase in oil exports and the foreign debt were considered resources in the approach to foreign disequilibrium. Today, the only solution is to stimulate both internal and export growth—the first in order to hold on to currency, and the second in order to generate it. This process demands a structural change that can be realized only partially and in the long term. For this reason internal adjustments are limited in their efficacy, not because of domestic policies but because of the evolution of the international economy itself.

On the one hand, the rates of exchange for Mexico's natural resources, such as oil, are deteriorating: Prices have fallen from $40 a barrel in 1980 to less than $15 in 1986, when Mexico will receive $6,000 million less than in 1985 for the same 1.5 million barrels it exports every day. On the other hand, the rates of exchange for international capital financing with regard to other assets, goods, and services are being reevaluated because of the high cost of money. In international markets the nominal interest rates are between 9 and 10 percent, which in real terms means rates of 5–6 percent if we take into account an inflation rate of 3–4 percent. In the payment of debt service, these indices suppose expenditures of two or three times more resources than if the traditional real interest rates of 2 percent prevailed; that is, we find ourselves paying $5,000–6,000 million more than normal in the historical pattern of financial markets.

If we lose $6,000 million in oil income and pay $6,000 million more in servicing our foreign debt, the only solution (other than decreasing imports and curbing growth) is to compensate for this decline in receipts of foreign currency with more exports. In addition to the fundamental obstacle of time (for industrial reconversion is partial and long term), this situation confronts the problem of neoprotectionism in our principal export markets. The United States with a trade deficit of $150,000 million, Europe with an unemployment rate of 10–11 percent, and Japan with 75–100 percent of its economic growth based on increased foreign demand (exports) continue and deepen protectionism in practice despite their political speeches about free trade in international forums.

It is precisely in this context of crisis in the world economy that we must judge the measures recently announced by the Mexican government on February 21, 1986, to deal with the oil crisis. These ongoing measures are of both domestic and foreign scope, as follows:

1. In the domestic arena the *strategy for structural change* deepens and accelerates but does not change, given that the fundamental problems still remain.
2. The strategy is not modified, but there are *ongoing adjustments in domestic economic policy,* especially in the areas of balance of payments, rates of exchange, monetary policy and credit, trade, and foreign investment.
3. Finally, in the area of international negotiations, "it is necessary to *reformulate, in the light of new circumstances, our policies concerning our foreign debt, additional financing, and trade relations.*"

These proposals correspond exactly to the difficulties facing the national economy with regard to the international economic crisis, and they provide an integrated response to that crisis. The first two proposals attempt to generate the conditions that in the long and short terms will allow us to reduce and overcome our vulnerability in the face of an unstable world economy. The third opens the way to international negotiations in an effort to modify their asymmetrical tendencies, thus reaffirming the thesis that world problems and their solutions are the legitimate responsibility of all countries.

The principles of sovereignty and independence that underly our foreign policy and the principles of democracy and liberty that uphold our domestic policy are not subject to international economic negotiations. In response to this challenge to improve Mexico's economic dilemma and guard our sovereignty, the president said " . . . no one can remain outside the great battle we are waging. We are committed in all sectors: we must take our places in the battle for the Nation."

Thus, the problems stemming from the international oil crisis and our foreign petrodependence, the crisis in the international monetary system and the foreign debt, and the crisis in world trade and neoprotectionism constitute an interdependent trinomial whose solution will determine whether or not we overcome the current crisis in the national economy.

The International Oil Crisis and Mexico's Foreign Petrodependence

The International Crisis

The current trend in the international price of oil stems from actions taken simultaneously in economies that are high consumers of hydrocarbons and in the principal exporting countries of crude oil. These actions resulted from the aftermath of the 1970s price explosion that raised the barrel price more than 1,000 percent. In short, whereas a few years ago the petroleum market was a purveyor's or seller's market, today it belongs to the buyers.

At present, the petroleum industry is witnessing not only a crisis in its own market but also a restructuring of the international petroleum industry that has led to the classic problem of deterioration in the rates of exchange for Mexico's raw materials. The disarticulation of market forces motivated by the political strategy of the principals on both sides has accentuated this crisis.

Underlying the fall in international demand was an economic recession that has not yet been overcome, followed by industrial redeployment in the developed nations where petroleum began to be replaced both as a fuel and as an industrial investment. But, more important than the economic recession, the explanation for the decline in absolute consumption of crude oil should be sought in the modification of the bases for economic growth currently in effect in branches of industry that consume less energy. This modification limits the expansion of demand for oil to an annual median rate of 1–2 percent for the rest of the decade and to a rate not much higher than that until the end of the century. During the first price explosion (1973-1974) world consumption continued to rise, but during the second (1979-1980) it began to decrease—ultimately, from 52.4 million barrels a day to 45.3 million in 1985.

Supply, for its part, has increased. It has thus given rise to displacement in the production centers of the Middle East and to atomization of supply, as a result of the large number of independent producers encouraged by the high price of crude oil in the 1970s. Some nations moved only toward self-sufficiency, while others became genuine exporters; only a few reached the prominence of Mexico, Great Britain, Norway, Egypt, and Malaysia, the new powers in the market.

The current world oversupply of petroleum is reflected not only in the 2.5 million barrels a day that find no place in the market but also in the unused installed capacity of more than 13 million barrels a day.

Moreover, the spot market increased its participation in the world supply until it became The Market itself, which then generated the futures market and the system of netbacks by refineries—a system that, in turn, has reduced contractual buying and selling.

Faced with this panorama of falling prices and consumption, OPEC recently changed its strategy from defending prices to defending its participation in the world market, thereby unleashing the war against certain independent producers unwilling to cooperate in favor of stabilization. As Miguel de la Madrid stated in his Message to the Nation on February 21, 1986, "The diligent and ongoing efforts that Mexico has made during the past three years to avoid this situation achieved some results during the first two years, but beginning with the second half of 1985 we have been faced with the insuperable problem of lack of comprehension and lack of will to achieve stability and order in the petroleum market."

Thus, the objective situation of a falling market was exacerbated by a price war with unpredictable consequences in which no free play of supply and demand could return equilibrium to the market. The price of oil came under the control of its consumers, just as it continues to be controlled by them at present.

Mexico's Foreign Petrodependence

In this context it is important to keep clearly in mind the nature of the foreign vulnerability of the Mexican economy with respect to petroleum. Although the situation has various ramifications, the reference here is not to the petrolization of the Mexican economy but rather to its foreign petrodependence.

Mexico is the fourth largest petroleum producer in the world, with a daily production of 2.7 million barrels and an average daily exportation of 1.5 million barrels. But petrolization does not occur in Mexico because hydrocarbons represent only 10 percent of the total national production of goods and services; the remaining 90 percent consists of nonpetroleum goods and services. (In other countries, such as Venezuela, the production of hydrocarbons constitutes 30–40 percent; in Saudi Arabia such production has reached 90 percent.) Therefore, it has been said that Mexico is "more than oil"; indeed, we must find our own mechanism for extricating ourselves from the international oil crisis given the 90 percent of national production devoted to nonpetroleum goods and services.

If petrolization of the economy is not occurring, then we must determine just what has caused our vulnerability problem. The question is threefold and touches on trade, finance, and fiscal policy: (1) Regarding *monoexportation,* petroleum exports represent 75 percent of the total sale of goods that Mexico realizes abroad. (2) Regarding *financial monodependence of currency,* petroleum has generated almost 50 percent of the income in foreign currency derived from goods and services. And (3) regarding *fiscal dependence,* taxes on hydrocarbons represent more than 50 percent of fiscal income, of which almost 40 percent comes from payments of export taxes by PEMEX. In other words, the petroleum industry, which generates only 10 percent of the national product, contributes more than half of our fiscal income.

The reasons for these three phenomena must be sought in the relations maintained by the national petroleum industry with other economic sectors in recent decades. In the 1970s, for instance, petroleum operations increased almost tenfold and maintained a comparable increasing importance in the total national economy. Although industrial production doubled, no progress was made in the articulation of productive sectors and in the industrialization of capital goods and exports; as a result, the demand for imports was heightened. Foreign indebtedness was used to close the gap between imports and exports and to complement domestic savings. In this way, the foreign debt was increased in 1980 to 1986 from $20,000 million to $80,000 million. Moreover, imports of manufactured goods rose to $60,000 million between 1978 and 1981, whereas exports reached only $14,000 million; hence the trade deficit in manufacturing reached $46,000 million and could not be covered even by the total income from the export of hydrocarbons during this period ($32,000 million).

Thus it could be said that petroleum and the foreign debt were used not to correct the foreign trade deficit in manufacturing but to finance it. The structural change in industry and foreign trade was postponed, resulting in monoexportation.

Domestic and International Solutions

Faced as it is with this situation, Mexico must move ahead with concrete measures that will allow it to overcome the phenomenon of monoexportation on the domestic front and help to set rational parameters in the international market. In order to achieve these goals, it must continue, deepen, and accelerate the strategy of structural change in order to reverse the problem of disarticulation between industry and foreign trade. Mexico cannot move past monoexportation simply by promoting exports; it must take actions that will favor the strengthening of a nonintensive endogenous sector (basic consumer goods and widely distributed investments) in currency capable of promoting national development and creating an exporting sector that can maintain and increase its presence in international markets.

Foreign Petrodependence Calls for Structural Change

Fiscal vulnerability indicates the need to reverse the disproportionate contribution of petroleum to government income. In an attempt to achieve this goal, the segments of the 90 percent share of the economy that is nonpetroleum must collaborate in establishing sectoral and social equity so that those who have more will pay more. As President de la Madrid stated in his message of February 21, 1986: "In the area of taxation we will increase our collection efforts and the law will be strictly enforced with regard to evaders. At the opportune moment we will propose the changes necessary to better adapt the tax structure to current economic reality through fiscal measures that will give to the State the resources it needs to fulfill the tasks that society demands of it."

In the international arena it will not be the "invisible hand" of the free market that balances the situation, because the petroleum market is controlled as much by quantities as by prices and the impetus of the petroleum market is not merely the simple security rate.

Mexico must deepen both its active policy of cooperation and its effort to coordinate measures to end uncertainty; it must also return a certain amount of stability to the world hydrocarbon market. It is imperative that, without diminishing our sovereignty, we contribute to the effort organized by the oil-exporting nations whose interests coincide with our own.

The fall in prices has worsened the economic situation in Mexico, a country that finds itself in a critical period such that payment of debt service is implicitly conditioned by petroleum income. This situation does not exist in Mexico alone, however. Several nations that export oil and import capital find themselves trapped by this dialectic; moreover, the current financial crises in Algeria, Ecuador, Egypt, Indonesia, Malaysia, and Venezuela have opened for negotiation the restatement of guidelines for the international financial system.

The Crisis in the International Financial System and the Foreign Debt

Another fundamental aspect of the vulnerability of the Mexican economy is the magnitude of the accumulated foreign debt, which has derived both from the procedures of the international financial system and from disequilibrium. The international financial system, founded in 1944, granted to the dollar a dual role: as medium of the international reserve, with a fixed parity to gold, and as the national currency of the United States. It was this dual role that stimulated growth in the 1950s and 1960s along with stable prices and interest rates. In the 1970s, following Nixon's decision regarding the nonconvertibility of the dollar for gold and the establishment of flexible types of exchange, the North American government issued larger quantities of money with which it generated an international superliquidity that allowed it to export its inflation. Toward the end of the decade the strategy was inverted; in order to stimulate economic recovery with low rates of inflation, and in order to finance the fiscal deficit, the real interest rates rose above the historical rates of 2 percent until they reached an annual average of 6–7 percent.

As a result of these policies, the dollar was strengthened by 30–40 percent and high interest rates became the axis of North American economic strategy in response to the lack of cooperation by member states of the Organization for Economic Cooperation and Development (OECD).

Thus, high interest rates attract capital to the United States from Europe, Japan, and the developing countries, which finance the United States' $200,000 million national debt. For the developing nations this situation signifies an increase in debt service and strong currency flight, both of which contribute to the insolvency of these nations and accentuate the spiral of indebtedness.

Moreover, the overvaluation of the dollar has given impetus to the United States' trade deficit of more than $150,000 million, thus supposing a loss of confidence in that currency as a reserve asset; however, the political will to keep the currency high conforms to the goal of holding up the "Currency God" even if that means sacrificing the system of production.

One of the causes for the superindebtedness of the developing nations is the traditional foreign imbalance of these economies, which is derived in turn from the disarticulated process of replacing imports and from the indiscriminate use of foreign funds whose utilization in financing development was accentuated during the second half of the past decade.

It was the coincidence between the need to resort to debt and the international superliquidity that shot up the volume of banking credit. And it was the debt service in the face of unprecedented real interest rates that precipitated the indebtedness crisis.

Until 1978 the cost of money was only half of what it would become years later when the prime rate reached a historic peak of 20.5 percent. Beginning in 1982 the debtor nations became genuine exporters of capital; between 1982 and 1985 Latin America exported $105,000 million in interest and services and received only $18,000 million, exclusive of the persistent currency flight.

In short, Mexico has fallen into debt as a result of internal problems. It has been lent money because of international superliquidity. The crisis of indebtedness has been faced by means of unilateral adjustment by the debtor nations, when in fact the responsibility for the problem and its solution should be shared equally. If some countries went into debt "irresponsibly," it was because they found creditors who were equally "irresponsible."

Mexico's efforts to adjust the economy have been significant ever since the first restructuring of the foreign debt in August 1982. From 1980 to 1985 alone, it has paid $77,732 million in interest and amortization. Moreover, the policy of adjustment has translated into enormous sacrifices for the people. In the current situation, the persistence of high interest rates and the deterioration in terms of exchange, both of which were sharply evident in the sudden drop in oil prices, mean that our country will be unable to continue meeting the exaggerated amounts required to service the debt.

Previously, Mexico had pointed to the need for a new formula for renegotiating its foreign debt, and today the criteria that should guide this formula have been defined. The following must be taken into account: adjustment of the debt service to the country's real ability to pay; reliance on efficient mechanisms for financing and reducing the cost; awareness of Mexico's capacity for growth and repayment; and an international atmosphere that favors cooperation in the different areas of the world economy.

Mexico has always opted for, and will continue opting for, an international policy of negotiation, cooperation, and rejection of confrontation; however, as former Secretary of the Interior Jesus Silva Herzog has indicated, if the creditors persist in their inflexibility, Mexico will opt for unilateral measures.

In this connection, the recent Agreement on Expanded Facilities was signed with the IMF; for the first time this body recognized the need for economic growth as a condition for debt payment in a developing country.

Until now, the IMF programs for domestic adjustment had allowed the creation of temporary surpluses in the balance of payments and the payment of debt service, but always at the expense of growth; in other words, the adjustment was made by means of recession. This time, however, the IMF has not only taken into account the overwhelming need for economic recovery, for which the Mexican government deems necessary a moderate rate of growth on the order of 3–4 percent a year, but it has also accepted fluctuations in the price of crude oil on the petroleum markets as a variable on which the success of the program and our nation's ability to pay both depend.

In the letter of intent that Mexico sent to the IMF and that served as the basis for the new agreement for the period 1986–1987, the Mexican government stated the difficulties its economy has experienced in recent years. These are summarized as follows. During the previous Agreement in Expanded Facilities covering the period 1983–1985, inflation was finally slowed, the public-sector deficit was substantially reduced despite increasing interest payments, and the balance of payments was strengthened. Still, economic contraction occurred in 1982 and 1983, followed by a slight turnaround in growth during 1984 and 1985. Interest payments higher than those programmed for, the lack of foreign financing, the impact of the decline in international petroleum markets, and the earthquakes of September 1985 created pressures on the balance of payments and adversely affected economic recovery.

In the same letter, Mexico agreed not only to implement additional corrective measures in the public-sector deficit but also to strengthen the balance of payments, reduce inflation, and continue the rationalization of the public sector in order to allow greater channeling of resources to the private sector. In other words, Mexico must adopt a new economic program oriented toward growth and realize certain necessary structural reforms, which in turn will require internal strengthening of public finances and fresh financial resources from abroad, estimated at about $11,000–12,000 million from now until the end of 1987.

The new program would incorporate a special mechanism that relates variations in the price of oil to growth goals. If the average price remains between $9 and $14 a barrel, foreign financing will not be modified. If the price falls below $9 a barrel, a nine-month period of protection will ensue, in which additional foreign financing will match every dollar that falls in price, on a one-to-one basis; after this period, the plan would incorporate internal adjustments. If the price rises above $14 a barrel, foreign financing would be reduced in proportion to the additional income.

A second special mechanism deals with guaranteed growth and would go into effect if recovery does not occur. In this case, when an increase is foreseen in public investment in high-yield projects that would use domestic materials rather than large quantities of imports, investment by the private sector would be encouraged. Financing this mechanism would require additional aid from credit institutions and the internal bank estimated at $500 million.

We must recognize, however, that although the new agreement represents substantial progress in the IMF's understanding of the problems that beset the Mexican economy, the support of the international financial community is also necessary. The success of the program would require creditors to take into consideration Mexico's dependence on and vulnerability to variations in oil prices, and to make an effort to reestablish normal practices in the financial market so as to make the voluntary credit of commercial banks available once again.

The Crisis in International Trade and Neoprotectionism

If the increase in petroleum exports and the foreign debt are no longer the sources of currency needed to finance Mexico's foreign deficits, the only way to continue importing the capital goods and industrial investments that growth requires is to export nonpetroleum products. Hence the importance of observing the evolution of international trade and its impact on the Mexican economy.

Three problems are associated with the opening of international markets today: recession in the industrialized nations, deterioration of the rates of exchange for our raw materials, and the rise of neoprotectionism.

In recent years international trade has witnessed a declining trend; now it is no longer the impetus to growth that it had been in the postwar era. During the 1960s the exports of manufactured goods increased to 9 percent in annual volume, and in the 1970s a substantial decrease occurred in exported volumes, with an annual growth rate of only 2–3 percent. This trend continued into the early 1980s, reaching its lowest level in 1982, when exportation contracted for the first time in thirty years. Between 1983 and 1986, its behavior has been erratic, varying according to the number of markets that were open.

The principal reason for the deterioration in world trade has undoubtedly been the stagnating economy in the industrialized nations and developing economies. A direct relationship exists between economic growth and trade in goods. Thus, for example, an annual increase of 4 percent in the industrialized countries correspond to an expansion of trade amounting to 8 percent between 1950 and 1975. In other words, the world economic recession that began in the 1970s led to a significant decrease in the volume of goods traded; at the same time this decrease constituted a real restraint on industrial recovery.

This problem has been heightened by the neoprotectionist policies of the industrialized nations in effect since the mid-1970s. In fact, owing to a variety of internal cuases, these countries have adopted such policies even when they continue to state their support of a free market. As an example of the effects that protectionist measures other than tariffs can have, one need only consult the estimates made by the United Nations Conference for Trade and Development (UNCTAD). These estimates indicate that if the tariffs were removed from 150 key products exported by Third World countries, their incomes would be raised by $35,000 million a year—an amount almost two-fifths of the debt service that these countries will owe in 1985.

The United States, for instance, has had recourse to neoprotectionism as a measure to counteract its problems of low industrial productivity in comparison to Europe and Japan. In addition, its high trade deficit has been the result of a supervaluation in the rate of exchange caused by a policy of high interest rates.

Europe, for its part, has had recourse to neoprotectionism in its desire to hold onto currency that will allow it to create domestic jobs in an effort to combat its high unemployment rate—between 10 and 11 percent of the working-age population.

Japan's low rate of domestic consumption and high levels of savings mean that its production is oriented abroad, thus severely limiting a more dynamic trade exchange. Japan's economic growth is explained almost exclusively by the increase in foreign demand and exports in recent years.

In reality, world trade is moving closer and closer to a situation involving trade in controlled markets, especially in the productive centers of steel, automobiles, shoes, and textiles. As Boyd France has pointed out, only 20 percent of the volumes exchanged in the world conform to the rules of the General Agreement on Tariffs and Trade (*Business Week*, January 27, 1986).

Moreover, the developing countries have experienced a decrease in their currency income because of the steep drop in the price of raw materials, which in turn has given rise to a deterioration in the terms of trade exchange. Between 1981 and 1985 the terms of exchange in foreign trade for Latin America deteriorated by 16.5 percent. In 1985 alone, $15,000 million were transferred in this way to developed economies.

By the same token, sugar-exporting Third World countries lost income derived from this product estimated at more than $7,000 million in

1983, and, at present, because of the fall in oil prices, Mexico's income for 1986 has been reduced by an estimated $6,000 million.

According to the Economic Commission for Latin America (CEPAL), the volume of products traded in 1985 fell 3 percent and the volume of Latin American exports was reduced 2 percent last year, thus marking the first negative variation since 1975. Moreover, the combined effect of lowered prices and volumes in 1985 was responsible for a drop in Latin American exports of some 5.7 percent, which represents a total of $5,580 million.

With this outline in mind, we are able to analyze the behavior of Mexican foreign trade. Corresponding to a highly favorable international context characterized by a type of fixed exchange and inflation and interest rates between 1 and 2 percent was a stage in the Mexican economy described as stabilizing development in the decade of the 1960s. However, the breakdown of the Bretton Woods system and the petroleum crisis in the early 1970s were determining factors in the decreased rate of growth in the Mexican economy. This decrease was temporarily alleviated in the late 1970s thanks to Mexico's new status as an oil-exporting nation during a period when prices reached their highest levels. From the beginning, the replacement of imports was accompanied by a fundamental problem for industrial development in Mexico—the traditional trade deficit in manufactured goods resulting from high dependence on foreign economies for capital goods and investments to maintain growth.

One of the solutions to Mexico's foreign trade deficit would be to substantially improve the exchange relations with our principal partner— that is, to have greater participation in the purchases made by the United States abroad (3-4 percent of the North American market). Other options would emerge from trade integration with Latin American countries, which can be achieved in the absence of dollars by means of unconventional trade agreements such as barter.

In sum, today's economies are more interdependent on international economic activity than those of the past. And Mexico's foreign vulnerability is greater in the 1980s than it was before. Strategy and viable economic policies are necessary to overcome the crisis, but they are not enough to counteract the international crises that persist in the oil industry, in finance, and in trade. It is necessary, therefore, to deepen Mexico's active international policy in all forums of international cooperation, and to encourage the international community to share equally in the cost of the crisis.

Appendix A
PEMEX Financial Statistics

United Mexican States
1982-1984 Results and Main Economic Policy Goals and Projections

	1982	1983	1984	1985[a]
A) Real GDP (annual % change)	-0.5	-5.3	3.5	3.5
B) Consumer price index (December-December)	98.8	80.8	59.2	35.0
C) Gross domestic investment (% of GDP)	21.0	16.0	16.4	16.9
D) Public sector deficit (% of GDP)	17.9	8.5	6.0	4.3
E) Banco de Mexico's reserves (U.S. millions)	1,832.3	4,933.1	8,134.0	9,762.0
F) Current account balance (U.S. billions)	-4.9	5.5	4.1	1.5
(% of GDP)	-3.0	3.8	2.3	0.8
G) Trade balance (U.S. billions)	6.8	13.7	13.6	10.7
Export	21.2	21.4	23.7	24.4
Imports (FOB)	14.4	7.7	10.1	13.7
H) Interest payments on external debt (U.S. billions)	11.3	9.8	11.8	10.8
I) Effective interest rate on external debt (%)	13.2	10.9	12.4	10.9
J) Net external financing (U.S. billions)	7.2	4.7	2.4	0.4

[a]Projected

Proven Reserves (millions of barrels)

	1982	1983	1984
Crude and natural gas liquids	56,998	57,096	56,410
Natural gas (equivalents of crude oil)	15,010	15,404	15,340
Total	72,008	72,500	71,750

Probable reserves: 58,650

Potential reserves: 250,000

Exports of Crude Oil by Geographic Distribution (in percentage)

Country	1982	1983	1984
United States	49.9	48.3	49.1
Spain	11.4	10.8	10.9
Japan	7.6	7.9	9.8
England	5.6	5.9	4.9
France	5.7	6.5	5.1
All Others	20.8	20.6	20.2
Total	100.0	100.0	100.0

Mexico's Five-Year Plans (1985-1989)

Sources and Uses of Foreign Exchange (millions of dollars)

	1985	1986	1987	1988	1989	1985-1989
Revenues	15,961.9	16,401.9	16,263.5	16,974.4	17,564.2	83,165.9
Operating expenses and capital expenditures	1,524.1	2,080.4	2,205.0	2,366.1	2,520.8	10,696.4
Interest	2,241.0	2,089.7	2,113.6	2,120.5	2,099.4	10,664.2
Debt retired	994.0	425.0	522.6	639.6	795.3	3,376.5
Other expenses	661.1	768.2	648.5	928.4	727.6	3,733.8
Net contribution to the rest of the economy	10,541.7	11,038.6	10,773.8	10,919.8	11,421.1	54,695.0

Financial Structure (in percentage)

	1985	1986	1987	1988	1989
Total assets	100.0	100.0	100.0	100.0	100.0
Equity	60.0	63.0	68.0	70.0	72.0
Surplus due to revaluation	34.0	35.0	41.0	48.0	50.0
Leverage Total debt/equity (%)	0.7	0.6	0.5	0.4	0.4

Sources: Petroleos Mexicanos, Second Evaluation Meeting, 1983-85 (Mexico, January 28, 1986); and Petroleos Mexicanos, Financial Presentation, 1985.

Appendix B
Inter-American Development Bank,
External Debt and Economic Development in Latin America: Excerpts from "Mexico" (Washington, D.C.: IDB, 1983), pp. 176–179.

Mexico: Structure of the Public Sector, 1970, 1975, 1976, and 1980 (percentages)

	1970		1975		1976		1980	
	Revenues	Expendi-tures	Revenues	Expendi-tures	Revenues	Expendi-tures	Revenues	Expendi-tures
General government	46.0	49.8	39.9	47.5	45.1	51.6	45.0	46.0
Federal government[a]	41.3	45.1	35.8	43.7	40.7	47.6	41.3	41.5
Federal district department	4.7	4.7	4.1	3.8	4.4	4.0	3.7	4.5
Public enterprises and decentralized agencies (budgetary)	54.0	50.2	60.1	52.5	54.9	48.4	55.0	54.0
PEMEX	20.1	14.3	17.4	13.0	19.2	13.4	29.1	25.7
Others	33.9	35.9	42.7	39.5	35.7	35.0	25.9	28.3
Consolidated public sector[b]	100.0	100.0	100.0	100.0	100.0	100.0	100.0	100.0
(percent of gross domestic product)	18.8	20.5	23.6	31.5	23.7	30.3	31.4	37.4

[a]Adjusted not to duplicate the Federal Government transfers.
[b]Includes Federal Government, 16 budgetary agencies and D.D.F. (excluding the subway).
Source: J.L.P., *Primer Informe de Gobierno*, Annex I-1977, pp. 138-142, J.L.P., *Quinto Informe de Gobierno*, Annex I-Historical Statistics, 1981, pp. 195-199.

Size and Structure of the Public Sector

During the 1970's, the size of the Mexican public sector increased dramatically as new programs and institutions were formed as part of the Echeverría expansionist policy aimed at socio-economic redistribution. This was to be achieved through social parameters and economic growth as well as through agricultural and industrial investment to expand the productive centers.

The Mexican public sector includes the general government and public enterprises. The general government is comprised of the Federal Government, two social security institutions, 31 state governments, the Federal District, over 30 decentralized agencies, and more than 2,300 municipalities. The most important state enterprises are the state petroleum corporation (PEMEX), the food marketing and price stabilization board (CONASUPO), the railroads and the electricity corporation.

The relative size of the general government in terms of revenue and expenditure has been consistently less than half of the consolidated public sector. In terms of overall size, PEMEX is unquestionably outstanding. Of the total revenue generated by state enterprises, PEMEX contributed 30 percent in 1977 and 50 percent in 1981. Furthermore, PEMEX contributes an increasing portion of Federal Government tax revenue due to its high taxation rates, amounting to 4 percent of GDP (or roughly one quarter of total tax revenue) in 1981.

Beginning in 1972, the Government initiated a program of public economic expansion through a marked increase in capital expenditure, resulting in an overall deficit of 4.1 percent of GDP in that year. From this point on, capital expenditure comprised over 7 percent of GDP in each year during the 1972–82 period.

Capital expenditure priorities were concentrated fixed investment, particularly agricultural and industrial investment. The agricultural sector received 15.9 percent of total public expenditure in 1975 compared to 8.8 percent in 1970. Rural development programs in particular received increased budget allocations. The functional classification of expenditure is shown in the Appendix.

At the same time, revenue mobilization was not sufficient to meet rising expenditures. In keeping in line with expansionary priorities, special tax credits were given to enterprises investing in industrial activities in underdeveloped regions. However, income tax collection was more strictly enforced, beginning in 1972, resulting in a 25 percent increase over the previous year. Within the Federal Government, tax revenue increased as a percentage of GDP from an average 8.5 for the 1970–72 period to an average 10.1 for the 1973–75 period.

Public sector revenue mobilization was hampered by the large degree of subsidization and price control of many goods and services produced by pubic enterprises. In the 1970–75 period the public enterprises experienced substantial operating losses, partially due to pricing and subsidization policies. As a result, federal government current transfers increased as a percentage of GDP from an average 3 percent for 1970–72 to over 4 percent of GDP for the 1973–75 period. The problem of price adjustments and subsidization of foodstuffs, electricity and petroleum products has continued to exacerbate public enterprise deficits as well as had other negative implications for the economy as a whole.

The resulting fiscal deficits in the 1973–75 period accounted for over 6 percent of GDP in each year, reaching over 9 percent in 1975. In the following year, the overall deficit position and current savings of the public sector improved slightly due to increases in tax collections and public enterprise receipts. The latter was attributable to the higher revenues of PEMEX which increased export volume as well as peso receipts after the devaluation.

On the expenditure side, 1976 marked the beginning of a slackening of both current and capital expenditures in real terms, principally due to a decrease in current and capital transfers. What investment did occur was shifted toward PEMEX, with the social sectors becoming a lower priority. As mentioned previously, the high tax rate imposed on PEMEX by the Federal Government[1]

---

[1]In 1977–1979 PEMEX tax payments totaled approximately 25 percent of its total revenue.

and the potential for increased foreign exchange earnings through petroleum exports led to the decision to invest heavily in the state enterprise. However, this created a revenue structure which would become highly vulnerable to world market prices for one particular commodity. Other public enterprises continued to experience operating losses due to mismanagement and the above-mentioned pricing difficulties.

In 1977, the López Portillo administration, initiated measures to increase public sector efficiency. An administrative reform was begun which included a general Public Debt Law giving the Ministry of Finance the sole power to authorize debt negotiations and to prepare an annual financing program for the public sector in accordance with national investment priorities. Furthermore, the external debt surveillance included government debt monitoring by the Congress as well as the establishment of a legislative advisory committee on Foreign Financing of the Public Sector to establish external borrowing guidelines.

Other administrative reform measures included the establishment of closer ties between investment priorities and actual expenditure execution through reviews by the pertinent ministries as well as an improvement of the budgetary allocation process.

Along with the administrative reform, a tax reform was initiated following the 1976 devaluation which was to continue into the eighties. The first stage included investment incentives to promote fixed capital formation, while later the tax base was redefined to consider global income, and the capital gains tax to include only real gains. By 1980 a new value added tax of 10 percent, a new income tax law, changes in the customs code and various smaller sales and consumption taxes were introduced.

These reforms were part of a stabilization program initiated to reverse the grave economic situation of the early seventies. Through the above-mentioned reforms, efforts to improve public enterprise management, and a restrained fiscal expenditure policy, current savings rose to over 2 percent of GDP in 1977 and reached 6.1 percent of GDP in 1979, the highest proportion since 1970.

The overall deficit also improved through 1978, although not as markedly due to expanded PEMEX operations. As increased production coincided with rises in international petroleum prices in 1979, PEMEX current revenue increased substantially and accounted for over half of non-general government public revenue by 1981.

Increased capital expenditure in 1979 was primarily directed toward expanding petroleum production capacity and resulted in a rise in the overall deficit. However, current account savings increased mainly due to increases in tax revenue and decreases in current expenditures, in spite of a substantial increase in transfers and subsidies.

Beginning in 1980, current expenditure in the public sector rose substantially. While the average current expenditure as a percentage of GDP for 1977–79 was 21.7, the 1980–1982 average was 30 percent. The overall deficit in 1980 increased only slightly in real terms over the previous year due to a sharp decrease in capital expenditure. However, current savings dropped sharply from over 6 percent of GDP to 2.6 percent, despite substantial increases in PEMEX earnings. In 1980 its operating surplus before taxes amounted to almost 5.8 percent of GDP.

While in 1980 increases in revenue were responsible for a current account surplus, the following year savings dropped to negative levels and the overall deficit almost doubled. This decline is attributable to decreasing revenue in real terms due to petroleum market prices, increasing capital expenditure especially by PEMEX, as well as growing transfers to the public enterprises due to their declining financial positions.

Furthermore, the public sector's growing debt was reflected in a sharp increase in interest payments which amounted to almost 3 percent of GDP in 1982 compared to less than 2 percent in 1980. Increases in capital transfers are particularly noteworthy. While from 1977 to 1980 capital transfers comprised less than 1 percent of GDP, in 1981 they amounted to 4 percent.

Appendix C
Morgan Guaranty Trust Company, International Economics Department, *World Financial Markets* (New York: Morgan Guaranty Trust Company, April-May 1986).

Mexico: Rate of Return Differential and Capital Flight

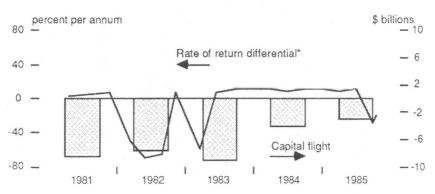

*Realized rate of return differential between Mexico and the United States on domestic CDs, adjusted for exchange rate changes.

Investment and Savings (percent of GNP in current prices)

	Investment[a]	Savings National	Savings Foreign[b]
Mexico			
1979-80 avg.	27.8	23.9	3.9
1981	30.0	24.8	5.2
1982	22.5	23.3	-0.8
1983	21.6	25.8	-4.2
1984	23.0	25.4	-2.4
1985	25.4	26.1	-0.7

[a]Gross fixed capital formation plus increase in stocks, except for Brazil where data on stocks are unavailable.
[b]Measured by the deficit on current account; minus sign indicates surplus.

Appendix D
Petróleos Mexicanos, *PEMEX Information Bulletin, 1986-1990: Petroleum Prices and Projections,* No. 33 (Washington, D.C.: PEMEX, June 1986).

PEMEX'S FINANCIAL RESULTS 1982-1985

LIABILITIES

Current liabilities	12.3	2.4	2.3	2.4	(80.5)
Long term liabilities	13.2	19.5	16.6	15.3	15.9
TOTAL Liabilities	25.5	21.9	18.9	17.7	(30.6)

EXPORTS AND IMPORTS OF OIL AND GAS PRODUCTS BY VOLUME

	1982	1983	1984	1985
EXPORTS				
Crude Oil (MBPD)	1'482	1'537	1'525	1'438
Refined products (MBPD)	42	84	111	136
Petrochemicals (tons per day)	2'392	2'208	1'579	931
Natural gas (MMCFPD)	260	217	148	-0-
IMPORTS				
Refined products (MBPD)	8	17	33	53
Petrochemicals (tons per day)	1'922	1'595	2'382	3'249
Natural gas (MMCFPD)	5	5	5	5

EXPORTS OF CRUDE OIL BY GEOGRAPHIC DISTRIBUTION (IN PERCENTAGE)

COUNTRY	1982	1983	1984	1985
United States	49.0	48.3	49.1	54.9
Spain	11.4	10.8	10.9	11.3
Japan	7.6	7.9	9.8	10.4
France	5.7	6.5	5.1	5.4
England	5.6	5.9	4.9	4.3
All others*	20.7	20.6	20.2	13.7
TOTAL	100.0	100.0	100.0	100.0

(Includes: Canada, Brazil, Uruguay, South Korea, Israel, Italy, San Jose Agreement, Austria, Taiwan and Portugal)

SUMMARY BALANCE SHEETS (IN BILLIONS OF DOLLARS)

ASSETS

	1982	1983	1984	1985	Average Increase 1985 Over 1982 %
Current assets	4.7	6.5	7.7	6.0	27.7
Fixed assets	29.5	31.8	36.4	30.6	3.7
TOTAL Assets	34.2	38.3	44.1	36.6	7.0

EQUITY

	1982	1983	1984	1985	
Certificates of Contribution and reserves	1.7	6.8	9.9	7.9	364.7
Surplus due to revaluation	7.0	9.6	15.3	11.0	57.1
Total Equity	8.7	16.4	25.2	18.9	117.2
TOTAL Equity and Liabilities	34.2	38.3	44.1	36.6	7.0
Exchange Rate For US $1.00	96.43	143.98	192.66	371.70	

SOURCES AND USES OF FOREIGN EXCHANGE (IN MILLIONS OF DOLLARS)

SOURCES

Collection from exports	15,307.5	16,101.0	18,597.7	15,163.4
Debt issued exports	12,113.3	352.2	99.5	382.6
Other income	102.9	63.7	99.3	66.5
TOTAL	27,523.7	16,516.9	16,796.5	15,582.4

USES

Goods and services used in operations	1,596.1	602.4	462.9	618.8
Capital expenditures	1,338.1	831.0	367.9	291.5
Interest	2,731.2	2,213.5	2,151.7	1,631.8
Paid-off debt	10,736.8	1,784.7	1,129.0	1,117.8
Other expenses	550.8	487.2	790.9	1,117.9
TOTAL	16,952.6	5,918.8	4,902.4	4,734.6
NET CONTRIBUTION TO THE REST OF THE ECONOMY	10,571.1	10,598.1	11,894.1	10,847.8

PROFILE OF PEMEX'S EXTERNAL DEBT

	DECEMBER 1984	DECEMBER 1985
Long-term debt	10,470.1	10,422.4
Bankers acceptances	3,940.5	3,315.4
Bond issues	1,128.1	1,183.4
Buyers credits	557.4	653.2
Leasing operations	301.6	273.1
TOTAL	16,397.7	15,847.5

PROFILE OF PEMEX'S EXTERNAL DEBT BY COUNTRY (IN MILLIONS OF DOLLARS)

DEBT BY COUNTRY	1984	%	1985	%
United States	3,693.6	22.5	3,460.8	21.8
Japan	2,995.9	18.3	2,801.2	17.7
Mexico	1,909.2	11.6	1,895.8	12.0
France	1,470.3	9.0	1,527.9	9.6
England	1,460.9	8.9	1,446.4	9.1
Canada	1,033.9	6.3	975.5	6.2
Germany	826.9	5.0	772.6	4.9
Luxemburg	688.5	4.2	695.2	4.4
Switzerland	596.8	3.6	588.0	3.7
Italy	407.2	2.5	381.9	2.4
Spain	312.8	1.9	310.3	2.0
Belgium	172.9	1.1	173.5	1.1
Brazil	147.4	0.9	142.3	0.8
Netherlands	109.5	0.7	105.6	0.7
Singapore	100.0	0.6	100.0	0.6
Other countries	470.9	2.9	470.7	3.0
TOTAL	16,397.7	100.0	15,847.5	100.0

Selected Bibliography: Mexico's Economic and Political Development

Gabrielle S. Brussel

Ackerman, C. *Mexico's Dilemma.* New York: Gordon Press Publishers, 1976.

Alba, Francisco. *The Population of Mexico: Trends, Issues and Policies.* New Brunswick, N.J.: Transaction Press, 1982.

Allub, Leopold, and Michel, Marco A., eds. *Impactos regionales de la politica petrolera en mexico.* Mexico City: Centroi de Investigacion para Integracion Social, 1982.

Archer, Jules. *Mexico and the United States.* New York: Hawthorn Books, 1973.

Astiz, Carlos Alberto, and McCarty, Mary F., comps. *Latin American Politics: Ambitions, Capabilities and National Institutions of Mexico, Brazil and Argentina.* Notre Dame, Ind.: University of Notre Dame, 1969.

Baerresen, Donald W. *The Border Industry's Program of Mexico.* Lexington, Mass.: Lexington Books/D. C. Heath, 1971.

Baird, Peter, and McCaughan, Ed. *Beyond the Border: Mexico and the U.S. Today.* New York: North American Congress on Latin America, 1979.

Barrett, J. *Mexico.* New York: Gordon Press Publishers, 1976.

Bazant, J. *A Concise History of Mexico from Hidalgo to Cárdenas, 1805-1940.* New York: Oxford University Press, 1977.

_____. *Alienation of Church Wealth in Mexico: Social and Economic Aspects of the Liberal Revolution, 1856-1875.* Edited and translated by Michael P. Casteloe. Cambridge: Cambridge University Press, 1971.

Belshaw, Michael Horace. *A Village Economy: Land and People of Huecario.* New York: Columbia University Press, 1967.

Benjamin, Thomas, and McNellie, William, eds. *Other Mexicos: Essays on Regional Mexican History, 1876-1911.* Albuquerque: University of New Mexico Press, 1984.

Bennett, Robert Lee. *The Financial Sector and Economic Development.* Baltimore, Md.: Johns Hopkins Press, 1965.

Brading, D. A. *Miners and Merchants in Bourbon Mexico, 1763-1810.* Cambridge: Cambridge University Press, 1971.

————. *Caudillo and Peasant in the Mexican Revolution.* Cambridge: Cambridge University Press, 1980.

Brandenburg, Frank. *The Making of Modern Mexico.* Englewood Cliffs, N.J.: Prentice-Hall, 1964.

Brenner, Anita, and Leighton, George R. *The Wind that Swept Mexico: The History of the Mexican Revolution, 1910–1942.* Austin: University of Texas Press, 1971.

Brocklehurst, Thomas U. *Mexico Today.* New York: Gordon Press Publishers, 1976.

Callahan, James M. *American Foreign Policy in Mexican Relations.* New York: Macmillan, 1932.

Camp, Roderic A. *The Making of a Government: Political Leaders in Modern Mexico.* Tucson: University of Arizona Press, 1984.

————. *Mexico's Leaders: Their Education and Recruitment.* Tucson: University of Arizona Press, 1980.

Camp, Roderic A., ed. *Mexico's Political Stability: The Next Five Years.* Boulder, Colo.: Westview Press, 1986.

Carrada Bravo, Francisco. *Oil, Money, and the Mexican Economy: A Macroeconometric Analysis.* Boulder, Colo.: Westview Press, 1982.

Chicano Studies Resource Center. *Mexico–United States Relations.* Los Angeles: University of California, 1983.

Cline, Howard F. *Mexico: Revolution to Evolution, 1940 to 1960.* 3rd edition. Westport, Conn.: Greenwood Press, 1981. Reprint of 1971 edition.

————. *U.S. and Mexico.* New York: Atheneum, 1963.

Cockroft, James D. *Mexico: Class Formation, Capital Accumulation and the State.* New York: Monthly Review Press, 1983.

————. *Intellectual Precursors of the Mexican Revolution, 1900–1913.* Austin: University of Texas Press, 1969.

Cornelius, Wayne A. *Politics and the Migrant Poor in Mexico City.* Stanford, Calif.: Stanford University Press, 1975.

Cosío Villegas, Daniel, ed. *Historia moderna de México.* México: Editorial Hermes, 1955–1977.

————. *El sistema político mexicano.* México: Joaquín Mortiz, 1972.

————. *El estilo personal de gobernar.* México: Joaquín Mortiz, 1974.

————. *La sucesión presidencial.* México: Joaquín Mortiz, 1975.

————. *Estados Unidos contra Porfirio Díaz.* México: Editorial Hermes, 1956.

————. *Memórias.* México: Joaquín Mortiz, 1973.

Crow, John Armstrong. *Mexico Today.* Revised edition. New York: Harper and Row, 1972.

Dabbs, Jack Autry. *The French Army in Mexico, 1861–1867.* The Hague: Mouton, 1963.

David, Jules. *American Political and Economic Penetration of Mexico.* Salem, N.H.: Ayer, 1976.

De Fornaro, Carlos. *Carranza and Mexico.* New York: Gordon Press Publishers, 1976.

De Walt, Billie R. *Modernization in a Mexico Ejido: A Study in Economic Adaptation.* Cambridge and New York: Cambridge University Press, 1979.

Diaz del Castillo, Bernal. *The History of the Conquest of New Spain.* New York: Penguin Books, 1958.

Dillon, Emile J. *Mexico on the Verge.* Salem, N.H.: Ayer, 1970. Reprint of 1921 edition.

Domínguez, Jorge I., ed. *Mexico's Political Economy: Challenges at Home and Abroad.* Beverly Hills, Calif.: Sage Publications, 1982.

Dulles, John W. *Yesterday in Mexico: A Chronicle of the Revolution, 1919-1936.* Austin: University of Texas Press, 1961.

Dunn, Frederick Sherwood. *The Diplomatic Protection of Americans in Mexico.* New York: Columbia University Press, 1933.

El Colegio de México. *Historia General de México.* 2 volumes, México: El Colegio de México, 1977-1981.

El Mallakh, R. *Petroleum and Economic Development.* Lexington, Mass.: Lexington Books/D. C. Heath, 1984.

Enock, C. *Mexico.* New York: Gordon Press Publishers, 1976.

Erb, Richard D., and Stanley R. Ross, eds. *United States Relations with Mexico: Concept and Content.* Washington, D.C.: American Enterprise Institute, 1981.

Fagen, Richard R., and Tuohy, William S. *Politics and Privilege in a Mexican City.* Stanford, Calif.: Stanford University Press, 1972.

Fehrenbach, T. R. *Fire and Blood: A History of Mexico.* New York: Macmillan, 1973.

Flores Caballero, Romeo. *Counterrevolution: The Role of the Spaniards in the Independence of Mexico, 1804-1838.* Translated by O. Rodriguez and E. Jaime. Lincoln: University of Nebraska Press, 1974.

Forsyth, Elizabeth R., and Ramírez, Gilberto, eds. *Development and Equity in Mexico: An Annotated Bibliography.* Austin: University of Texas Press, Mexico-U.S. Border Development Program, 1981.

Fox, Annette B. *The Politics of Attraction: Four Middle Powers and the United States.* New York: Columbia University Press, Institute of War and Peace Studies, 1977.

Frank, Andre Gunder. *Mexico's Agriculture: Transformation of the Mode of Production.* Cambridge and New York: Cambridge University Press, 1979.

Freithaler, William O. *Mexico's Foreign Trade and Economic Development.* New York: Praeger Publishers, 1968.

Fyfe, E. *The Real Mexico.* New York: Gordon Press Publishers, 1976.

Gentleman, Judith A. *Mexican Oil and Dependent Development,* Vol. 2. Chicago: University of Chicago Press, American University Studies (Political Science), 1978.

Gentleman, Judith A., ed. *Mexican Politics in Transition.* Boulder, Colo.: Westview Press, in press.

Gibson, Lay J., and Renteria, Alfonso C., eds. *The U.S. and Mexico: Borderland Development and the National Economies.* Replica Edition Series. Boulder, Colo.: Westview Press, 1985.

Gilderhus, Mark T. *Diplomacy and Revolution: U.S.-Mexican Relations Under Wilson and Carranza.* Tucson: University of Arizona Press, 1977.

Gilly, Adolfo. *The Mexican Revolution.* New York: Schocken Books, 1983.

Glade, William P., and Ross, Stanley P., eds. *Críticas constructivas del sistema político mexicano.* Encuesta Política México, No. 2. Austin: University of Texas Press, 1973.

González Casanova, Pablo. *Democracy in Mexico.* New York: Oxford University Press, 1970.

Gordon, Wendell C. *The Expropriation of Foreign Owned Property in Mexico.* Edited by Stuart Bruchey and Eleanor Bruchey. American Business Abroad Series. Salem, N.H.: Ayer, 1976. Reprint of 1941 edition.

Goulet, Denis. *Mexico: Development Strategies for the Future.* Notre Dame, Ind.: University of Notre Dame Press, 1983.

Grayson, George W. *The U.S. and Mexico: Pattern of Influence.* New York: Praeger Publishers, 1984.

––––––. *The Politics of Mexican Oil.* Latin American Series. Pittsburgh, Pa.: University of Pittsburgh Press, 1980.

Greene, Graham. *Another Mexico.* New York: Viking Press, 1981.

––––––. *The Lawless Roads.* New York: Penguin Books, 1947 and 1971.

Griffiths, Brian. *Mexican Monetary Policy and Economic Development.* New York: Praeger Publishers, 1972.

Grindle, Merilee S. *Bureaucrats, Politicians and Peasants in Mexico: A Case Study in Public Policy.* Berkeley: University of California Press, 1976.

Gruening, Ernest. *Mexico and Its Heritage.* Westport, Conn.: Greenwood Press, 1968. Reprint of 1940 edition.

Gutierrez de Lara, J., and Pinchon, Edgecumb. *The Mexican People: Their Struggle for Freedom.* New York: Gordon Press Publishing, 1976.

Guzman, Martin Luis. *The Eagle and the Serpent.* Translated by Harriet Onis. Gloucester, Mass.: Peter Smith Publishing Company, 1969.

Guzman, Oscar M., Yuñez-Naude, Antonio; and Wionczek, Miguel S. *Energy Efficiency and Conservation in Mexico.* Boulder, Colo.: Westview Press, 1986.

Hamilton, Nora. *The Limits of State Autonomy: Post-Revolutionary Mexico.* Princeton, N.J.: Princeton University Press, 1982.

Hanrahan, Gene Z. *Blood Below the Border: American Eye-Witness Accounts of the Mexican Revolution.* Chapel Hill, N.C.: Documentary Publications, 1982.

––––––. *Abajo, el Gringo! Anti-American Sentiment During the Mexican Revolution.* Chapel Hill, N.C.: Documentary Publications, 1982.

––––––. *The Murder of Madero and the Role Played by U.S. Ambassador Henry Lane Wilson.* Chapel Hill, N.C.: Documentary Publications, 1981.

––––––. *Documents on the Mexican Revolution.* Vols. 1–3. Chapel Hill, N.C.: Documentary Publications, 1976–1978.

Hanson, Roger D. *The Politics of Mexican Development.* Baltimore, Md.: Johns Hopkins University Press, 1971.

Hellman, Judith A. *Mexico in Crisis.* 2nd edition. New York: Holmes and Meier Publishers, 1983.

Hewlett, Sylvia, and Weinart, Richard, eds. *Brazil and Mexico: Patterns in Late Development.* Inter-American Politics Series. Philadelphia, Pa.: Institute for the Study of Human Issues, 1984.

Hodges, Donald Clark. *Mexico, 1910-1982: Reform or Revolution?* Westport, Conn.: Lawrence Hill, 1983.

Instituto Nacional de Estadística, Geografía e Informática. *Comparaciones internacionales México en el mundo, México 1985.* Mexico City: Instituto Nacional de Estadistica, Geografía e Informática, 1986.

International Bank for Reconstruction and Development. *World Debt Tables.* Washington, D.C.: World Bank, 1986.

James, Daniel. *Mexico and the Americans.* New York: Praeger Publishers, 1963.

Johnson, Kenneth. *Mexican Democracy: A Critical View.* Revised edition. New York: Praeger Special Studies, Praeger Publishers, 1978.

Johnson, W. W. *Heroic Mexico.* Revised edition. New York: Harcourt Brace Jovanovich, 1984.

Katz, Frederich. *The Secret War in Mexico: Europe, the United States and the Mexican Revolution.* Chicago: University of Chicago Press, 1981.

King, Timothy. *Mexico: Industry and Trade Policies Since 1940.* London and New York: Published for the Development Center of the Organization for Economic Co-operation and Development by Oxford University Press, 1970.

Kerr, Robert J. *A Handbook of Mexican Law.* New York: Gordon Press Publishers, 1976.

Koslow, Lawrence, ed. *The Future of Mexico.* Latin American Studies. Tempe: Arizona State University, 1976.

Kunz, Joseph K. *The Mexican Expropriations.* Millwood, N.Y.: Kraus Reprint, division of Kraus-Thomson Urgan, Ltd. Reprint of 1940 edition.

La Cascia, Joseph S. *Capital Formation and Economic Development in Mexico.* New York: Praeger Publishers, 1969.

Ladman, Jerry R. *U.S.-Mexican Energy Relationships: Realities and Prospects.* Lexington, Mass.: Lexington Books, 1981.

Ladman, Jerry R.; Baldwin, Deborah J.; and Bergman, Elihu. *U.S.-Mexican Energy Relationships.* Lexington, Mass.: D. C. Heath/Lexington Books, 1981.

Lamartine-Yates, Paul. *Mexico's Agricultural Dilemma.* Tucson: University of Arizona Press, 1981.

Levy, Daniel, and Székely, Gabriel. *Mexico: Paradoxes of Stability and Change.* Boulder, Colo.: Westview Press, 1983.

————. *Mexico: Profile of Stable Development.* Nations of Contemporary Latin America Series. Boulder, Colo.: Westview Press, 1982.

Lewis, Oscar. *The Children of Sánchez.* St. Paul, Minn.: Vintage Books, 1961.

————. *Five Families: Mexican Case Studies in the Culture of Poverty.* New York: Basic Books, 1959.

Liss, Peggy K. *Mexico Under Spain, Fifteen Twenty-One to Fifteen Fifty-Six: Society and the Origins of Nationality.* Chicago: University of Chicago Press, 1984.

Looney, Robert E. *Economic Policy-Making in Mexico.* Duke Press Policy Studies. Durham, N.C.: Duke University Press, 1984.

————. *Development Alternatives of Mexico Beyond the 1980's.* New York: Praeger Publishers, 1982.

————. *Mexico's Economy: A Policy Analysis with Forecast to 1990.* Boulder, Colo.: Westview Press, 1978.

Martin, P. *Mexico of the Twentieth Century,* 2 vols. New York: Gordon Press Publishers, 1976.

May, Herbert K. *Impact of Foreign Investment in Mexico.* Washington, D.C.: National Chamber Foundation, 1971.

McBride, Robert H., ed. *Mexico and the United States.* Englewood Cliffs, N.J.: Prentice-Hall, 1981.

McHenry, J. Patrick. *A Short History of Mexico.* Garden City, N.J.: Dolphin Books/Doubleday and Company, 1970.

Meier, M. S. *Bibliography of Mexican American History.* Westport, Conn.: Greenwood Press, 1984.

Meyer, Lorenzo. *Las empresas transnacionales en México.* México: El Colegio de México, 1974.

Meyer, Lorenzo, ed. *Mexico-estados unidos, 1982.* México: El Colegio de México, 1982.

Meyer, Michael C., and Sherman, William L. *The Course of Mexican History,* 2nd edition. New York: Oxford University Press, 1983.

Miller, R. R. *Mexico: A History.* Tulsa: University of Oklahoma Press, 1985.

Millor, Manuel. *Mexico's Oil: Catalyst for a New Relationship with the U.S.?* Boulder, Colo.: Westview Press, 1982.

Montgomery, Tommie Sue. *Mexico Today.* Philadelphia, Pa.: Institute for the Study of Human Issues, 1982.

Moorer, Thomas H., and Fauriol, George. *Caribbean Basin Security.* Washington Papers, No. 104. New York: Praeger Publishers, 1984.

Morales, Patricia. *Indocumentados mexicanos.* Mexico: Grijalbo, 1981.

Moreno Sanchez, Manuel. *Mexico: 1968–1972, crisis y perspectiva.* Austin: University of Texas Press, 1973.

Mosk, Sanford A. *Industrial Revolution in Mexico.* New York: Russell and Russell Books, division of Atheneum, 1975. Reprint of 1950 edition.

Needler, Martin. *Mexican Politics: The Containment of Conflict.* Edited by Robert Wesson. Politics in Latin America, a Hoover Institution Series. New York: Praeger Publishers, 1982.

———. *Politics and Society in Mexico.* Albuquerque: University of New Mexico Press, 1971.

Neumann, Peter H., and Cunningham, Maureen A. *Mexico's Free Textbooks— Nationalism and the Urgency to Educate.* Washington, D.C.: World Bank, 1982.

Newell, Robert, and Rubio, Luís. *Mexico's Dilemma: The Political Origins of Economic Crisis.* Special Studies on Latin America and the Caribbean. Boulder, Colo.: Westview Press, 1984.

Nicholson, Irene. *The Liberators: A Study of Independence.* New York: Praeger Publishers, 1969.

Ojeda, Mario. *Alcances y limites de la política exterior de México.* México: El Colegio de México, 1976.

Ojeda, Mario, ed. *Administración del desarrollo de la frontera norte.* México: El Colegio de México, 1982.

Ortiz Martínez, G. *Capital Accumulation and Economic Growth: A Financial Perspective on Mexico.* New York: Garland Publishing, 1984.

Padgett, L. Vincent. *The Mexican Political System*. New York: Houghton Mifflin, 1976.

Paz, Octavio. *The Labryinth of Solitude: Life and Thought in Mexico*. New York: Grove Press, 1961.

———. *The Other Mexico: Critique of the Pyramid*. New York: Grove Press, 1972.

Potash, Robert A. *Mexican Government and Industrial Development in the Early Republic: The Banco De Avio*. Amherst: University of Massachusetts Press, 1983.

Powell, T. G. *Mexico and the Spanish Civil War*. Albuquerque: University of New Mexico Press, 1981.

Purcell, Susan Kaufman. *The Mexican Profit-Sharing Decision*. Berkeley: University of California Press, 1976.

Purcell, Susan Kaufman, ed. *Mexico–United States Relations*, Vol. 34, No 1. New York: Academy of Political Science, 1981.

Quirk, Robert E. *Mexico*. Englewood Cliffs, N.J.: Prentice-Hall, 1971.

Raat, W. Dirk. *Mexico: From Independence to Revolution, 1881–1910*. Lincoln: University of Nebraska Press, 1982.

Ramos, Samuel. *Profile of Man and Culture in Mexico*. Austin: University of Texas Press, 1962.

Reyna, Jose Luis, and Weinert, Richard S., eds. *Authoritarianism in Mexico*. Inter-American Politics Series, Vol. 2. Philadelphia, Pa.: Institute for the Study of Human Issues, 1979.

Reynolds, Clark Winton. *The Mexican Economy: Twentieth Century Structure and Growth*. New Haven, Conn.: Yale University Press, 1970.

Riding, Alan. *Distant Neighbors: A Portrait of the Mexicans*. New York: Alfred A. Knopf, 1984.

Ross, John B. *The Economic System of Mexico*. Stanford: California Institute of International Studies, 1971.

Ross, Stanley. *Is the Mexican Revolution Dead?* New York: Alfred A. Knopf, 1966.

Ross, Stanley, ed. *Views Across the Border*. Albuquerque: University of New Mexico Press, 1978.

Ruíz, Ramón E. *The Great Rebellion: Mexico, Nineteen Hundred and Five to Nineteen Twenty-Four*. New York: Norton, 1980.

Russell, Thomas H. *Mexico in Peace and War*. New York: Gordon Press Publishers, 1976.

Ryan, John Morris. *Area Handbook for Mexico*. Washington, D.C.: Government Printing Office, 1970.

Samora, Julian. *Los Mojados: The Wetback Story*. Chicago: University of Chicago Press, 1971.

Sanders, Thomas Griffin. *Mexico in the 1970's*. Hanover, N.H.: American Universities Field Staff, 1975.

Schmitt, Karl Michael. *Mexico and the U.S., 1821–1973: Conflict and Coexistence*. New York: John Wiley and Sons, 1974.

Schmitter, Philipe C. *Mexico and Latin American Economic Integration*. Berkeley: University of California Press, Institute of International Studies, 1964.

Scholes, Walter V. *Mexican Politics During the Juarez Regime.* Columbia: University of Missouri Press, 1969.

Scott, Robert E. *Mexican Government in Transition.* Champaign-Urbana: University of Illinois Press, 1964.

Selby, Henry, and Murphy, Arthur D. *The Mexican Urban Household and the Decision to Migrate to the United States.* ISHI Occasional Papers in Social Change Series, No. 4. Philadelphia, Pa.: Institute for the Study of Human Issues, 1982.

Shafer, Robert J., and Mabry, Donald. *Neighbors—Mexico and the United States: Wetbacks and Oil.* Chicago: Nelson-Hall, 1984.

Sierra, Justo. *The Political Evolution of the Mexican People.* Translated by Charles Ramsdell. Austin: University of Texas Press, 1969.

Simpson, Lesley B. *Many Mexicos.* Berkeley: University of California Press, 1966.

Singer, Morris. *Growth, Equality and the Mexican Experience.* Austin: University of Texas Press, 1969.

Smith, Peter. *Labyrinths of Power: Political Recruitment in Twentieth Century Mexico.* Princeton, N.J.: Princeton University Press, 1979.

Smith, Peter H. *Mexico: Neighbor in Transition.* Headline Series. New York: Foreign Policy Association, 1984.

———. *Mexico: The Quest for a U.S. Policy.* New York: Foreign Policy Association, 1980.

Smith, Robert Freeman. *The United States and Revolutionary Nationalism in Mexico, 1916–1932.* Chicago: University of Chicago Press, 1972.

Solis, Leopoldo. *La realidad económica mexicano: retrovisión y perspectivas.* México: Siglo Veintiuno Editores, 1971.

———. *Economic Political Reform in Mexico: A Case Study for Developing Countries.* New York: Pergamon Press, 1981.

Stepan, Alfred C. "Mexico Deserves Full U.S. Attention." *New York Times,* June 17, 1986, p. A27.

Tannenbaum, Frank. *The Struggle for Peace and Bread.* New York: Columbia University Press, 1950.

Tello, Carlos, and Cordera, Rolando. *México: la Disputa por la nación.* México: Siglo XXI, 1981.

———. *La Política Económica Mexicana, 1970–1976.* México: Siglo XXI, 1979.

Thornburg, L. L. *Getting to Know Our Southern Neighbor.* New York: Vantage Press, 1984.

Toledo, Alejandro. *Petróleo y eco-desarrollo en el sureste de méxico.* México: Centro de Ecodesarrollo, 1982.

Trowbridge, E. D. *Mexico Today and Tomorrow.* New York: Gordon Press Publishers, 1976.

Tuck, J. *Pancho Villa and John Reed.* Tucson: University of Arizona Press, 1984.

Tucker, William Pierce. *The Mexican Government Today.* Minneapolis: University of Minnesota Press, 1957.

Turner, Frederick C. *The Dynamic of Mexican Nationalism.* Chapel Hill: University of North Carolina Press, 1968.

Turner, John Kenneth. *Barbarous Mexico.* Austin: University of Texas Press, 1969.

Tweedie, E. *Maker of Modern Mexico: Porfirio Diaz.* New York: Gordon Press, 1979.

Vásquez, Carlos, and Garcia y Griego, Manuel, eds. *Mexican-U.S. Relations: Conflict and Convergence.* UCLA Chicano Studies Research Center, UCLA Latin American Center. Los Angeles: University of California Press, 1983.

Velasco, Jesus-Augustin. *Impacts of Mexican Oil Policy on Economic and Political Development.* Lexington, Mass.: D. C. Heath/Lexington Books, 1983.

Vellinga, Menno. *Economic Development and the Dynamics of Class: Industrialization, Power and Control in Monterrey, Mexico.* Atlantic Highlands, N.J.: Humanities Press, 1979.

Vernon, Raymond. *The Dilemma of Mexico's Development: The Roles of the Private and Public Sectors.* Cambridge, Mass.: Harvard University Press, 1963.

Vernon, Raymond, ed. *Public Policy and Private Enterprise in Mexico.* Cambridge, Mass.: Harvard University Press, 1964.

Villarreal, René. *La contra-revolución monetarista.* Mexico: Oceano, 1982.

Walling, W. E. *The Mexican Question.* New York: Gordon Press Publishers, 1976.

Weber, David J. *Mexican Frontier: The American Southwest Under Mexico, 1821-1846.* Albuquerque: University of New Mexico Press, 1982.

Weintraub, Sidney. *Free Trade Between Mexico and the United States.* Washington, D.C.: Brookings Institution, 1984.

Weintraub, Sidney, ed. *Industrial Strategy and Planning in Mexico and the United States.* Boulder, Colo.: Westview Press, 1986.

Wilgus, A. Curtis. *Caribbean: Mexico Today.* Gainesville: University Presses of Florida, 1964.

Wilke, James W., et al., eds. *Contemporary Mexico: Papers of the Fourth International Congress of Mexican History.* Berkeley: University of California Press, 1976.

Winton, G. A. *A New Era in Old Mexico.* New York: Gordon Press Publishers, 1976.

Wionczek, Miguel S.; Guzman, Oscar M.; and Gutierrez, Roberto. *Energy Policy in Mexico: Prospects and Problems for the Future.* Boulder, Colo.: Westview Press, 1986.

Womack, John, Jr. *Zapata and the Mexican Revolution.* New York: Alfred A. Knopf, 1969.

Wright, Marie R. *Mexico: A History of Its Progress and Development in One Hundred Years.* New York: Gordon Press Publishers, 1979.

Wyman, Donald L., ed. *Mexico's Economic Crisis: Challenges and Opportunities.* Center for U.S.-Mexico Studies, Monograph Series No. 12. La Jolla: University of California Press, 1983.

Zbigniew, Anthony Kruszewski, and Richardson, William. *Mexico and the Soviet Bloc: The Foreign Policy of a Middle Power.* Boulder, Colo.: Westview Press, 1986.

About the Editor and Contributors

Mario Ramón Beteta. Lic. Mario Ramón Beteta has been Director General of Petróleos Mexicanos (PEMEX), Mexico's national oil industry, from 1982 to 1987. From 1976 to 1982 Lic. Beteta was Chairman and CEO of Banco Mexicano SOMEX, a state-owned industrial and financial conglomerate, and between 1965 and 1975 he served at the Ministry of Finance. Prior to that he served at Mexico's Central Bank (Banco de Mexico), for fifteen years. Lic. Beteta has been a Professor of Economics at the National University of Mexico, where he taught law and economics.

Gabrielle S. Brussel. Gabrielle Brussel is a graduate student in international political economy and Latin America at the School of International and Public Affairs at Columbia University. As research associate for the Puerto Rico Project at the Americas Society from 1982 to 1986, she was on the staff of the Western Hemisphere Commission on Public Policy Implications of Foreign Debt of the Americas Society. She was also Senior Research Associate of the Mexico Focus at the Americas Society. Her publications include contributions to *The Political Status of Puerto Rico* (1986) and *Brazil's Economic and Political Future* (Westview, forthcoming).

Guy F. Erb (Managing Director of Erb and Madian, Inc.). Guy Erb is Chairman of the U.S.-Mexico Policy Committee (Overseas Development Council U.S.-Mexico Project) and Chairman of the Trade and Investment Committee of the Mayor's International Advisory Council in Washington, D.C. Erb was a member of the National Security Council staff from 1977 to 1979, and in 1980 he was Deputy Director of the U.S. International Development Cooperation Agency and a member of the Board of Directors of the Inter-American Foundation. During the Kennedy Round, as a Foreign Service Officer, and during the Multilateral Trade Negotiations, Erb joined U.S. delegations to international trade negotiations.

Pamela S. Falk (Associate Director of the Institute of Latin American and Iberian Studies at Columbia University). Pamela Falk is associate professor of the adjunct faculty of Columbia University. She was formerly Associate Professor of international relations in the Political Science Department of Hunter College of the City University of New York, where she taught courses in Latin American foreign debt and international relations from 1979 to 1986. She was also director of Latin American Affairs at the Americas Society/Center for Inter-American Relations and Senior Adviser to its Western Hemisphere Commission on Public Policy Implications of Foreign Debt. She studied Spanish colonial history at the University of Madrid and received her Ph.D. from New York University. Dr. Falk's articles have been published in the *New York Times*, the *Los Angeles Times*, the *Wall Street Journal*, and the *New York Times Book Review*, among other journals. She is author of *Cuban Foreign Policy: Caribbean Tempest* and co-editor of *Brazil's Economic and Political Future* with Julian Chacel and David Fleischer (Westview, forthcoming, 1987). She is also editor of *The Political Status of Puerto Rico*. Dr. Falk is a member of the Council on Foreign Relations and serves on both the Board of Directors of the Caribbean Cultural Center and the National Advisory Council of the Center for the Study of the Presidency.

Edith Grossman. Edith Grossman, a critic and translator of Latin American literature, is the author of *The Antipoetry of Nicanor Parra*. Her work has appeared in various journals and publications, and she has translated many major Latin American writers, including Nicanor Parra, Mario Vargas Llosa, Julio Cortazar, Guillermo Cabrera Infante, and Jacobo Timmerman. Grossman teaches Spanish, humanities, and Latin American literature at Dominican College in Orangeburg, New York.

Alfredo Gutierrez Kirchner (General Representative, Petróleos Mexicanos [PEMEX]). Lic. Gutierrez Kirchner has served as General Representative for Petróleos Mexicanos (PEMEX) since 1978. From 1976 to 1978, he was General Director of Fiscal Administration of the Ministry of Treasury and Public Credit of Mexico; from 1971 to 1976 he was Executive Assistant to the President of the Inter-American Development Bank; and from 1960 to 1971, he served on several commissions within the Ministry of Treasury and Public Credit of Mexico. He was also Subdirector General of Revenue under the Ministry of Treasury and Public Credit of Mexico and has been a professor at several universities and academic centers.

Russell E. Marks, Jr. (Senior Vice President of Haley Associates). Russell Marks was the president and founding officer of the Americas Society. Before the formation of the society, Marks was president of Phelps Dodge International Corporation, which at that time had subsidiary and affiliate operations in fifteen countries including Mexico, Guatemala, Honduras, El Salvador, Costa Rica, Panama, Venezuela, Ecuador, and Chile (in Mexico the corporation had interests in several industries). Marks is a member of both the Council on Foreign Relations and the Board of Trustees of the American Academy of Dramatic Arts.

Edward L. Morse (Vice President, Petroleum Finance Company). Prior to joining the Petroleum Finance Company, Dr. Morse served as Director of International Affairs for the Phillips Petroleum Company. Before that, he served in the Department of State, first as Executive Assistant to the Under Secretary for Economic Affairs and, subsequently, as Deputy Assistant Secretary for International Energy Policy. Before his government service, Dr. Morse was the Executive Director of the "1980s Project," the largest research project in the history of the Council on Foreign Relations.

Susan Kaufman Purcell (Senior Fellow and Director, Latin American Project, Council on Foreign Relations). Dr. Purcell was a member of the Policy Planning Staff, U.S. Department of State, with responsibility for Latin America and the Caribbean. Before that, she served as an International Affairs Fellow at the Council on Foreign Relations. She has analyzed Latin America's investment climate, policymaking processes, and political outlook for several corporations, including Chase World Information Services, the Celanese Corporation, and Atlantic Richfield Corporation. From 1969 to 1981, Dr. Purcell was Assistant and later Associate Professor of Political Science at the University of California at Los Angeles. She has written extensively on Latin America, including an article on debt in *Foreign Affairs*.

Alan J. Stoga (Senior Associate, Kissinger Associates). Dr. Stoga was Vice President and head of the Country Risk Management Division of First National Bank of Chicago from 1977 to 1984 and an international economist at the U.S. Treasury Department from 1975 to 1977. He also served as chief Economic Consultant to the National Bipartisan Commission on Central America and, in 1983, was Special Commission Member Assistant to the Western Hemisphere Commission on Public Policy Implications of Foreign Debt of the Americas Society.

René Villarreal (Coordinator, Center of Project Evaluation and Promotion, Ministry of Energy, Mining, & Parastate Industry, Mexico). René Villarreal, in addition to his position as Coordinator General of the Center of Promotion and Project Evaluation at the Ministry of Energy, Mining, & Parastate Industry in Mexico, serves as Secretary of the Commission of Economic and Social Policy of the Institute of Economic, Political, and Social Studies at the PRI. Dr. Villarreal was Vice-Minister of Industrial and Commercial Planning in Mexico from 1982 to 1985. He taught economic theory and international trade at El Colegio de México and is author of numerous works including *La contrarevolución monetarista: Teoría, política económia y ideología de neoliberalismo* (The Monetarist Counterrevolution: Theory, Economic Policy, and Ideology of Neoliberalism). Dr. Villarreal received the Mexican government National Economic prize for his doctoral dissertation at Yale University, entitled "External Disequilibrium in the Industrialization of Mexico: A Structural Approach."

Index

Adjustment, 13–17, 69, 88, 94, 95.
  See also Stabilization programs
AFL-CIO (American Federation of
  Labor–Congress of Industrial
  Organizations), 45
Agreement on Expanded Facilities,
  94–96
Algeria, 92
Antidumping duties, 57
Argentina, 24, 48
Austerity, 31, 34, 59, 78
Automotive Decree, 42, 46

Baker, James, 24, 25
Baker Initiative, 24
Balance of payments, 10, 13(&
  table), 14, 16, 22, 23–24, 69,
  87, 95
Baldrige, Malcolm, 42
Banking
  expropriation of, 31, 44
  See also Credit, domestic
Bank of Mexico, 16
Beteta, Mario Ramón, 2
Bilateralism, 49–51, 52, 58. *See
  also* Reciprocity
Brazil, 48, 55
Bretton Woods system, 98

Cactua petrochemical complex, 74
Canada, 49, 50
Capital flight, 3, 11, 12, 13–15, 16,
  18, 21, 22, 24, 93, 105
Cárdenas, Lázaro, 1, 63, 66, 67, 70
Caribbean Basin Initiative, 49
Carter, Jimmy, 41
Central American crisis, 32–33, 94,
  98
Central Bank, 69
CEPAL. *See* Economic Commission
  for Latin America

CFE. *See* Federal Electricity
  Commission
Ciudad PEMEX, 74
Code on Subsidies and
  Countervailing Duties, 43, 58
Confederación de Trabajadores de
  México (CTM), 28, 66
Congrejera, La, 73
Conservation, 75
Consumer prices, 11(table), 15, 16,
  69. *See also* Inflation
Corruption, 15, 31–32
Countervailing duties, 43, 48, 57
Credit
  domestic, 16, 19, 20, 76
  foreign, 15, 16, 19, 23, 24, 94, 95
  See also Debt; National debt
CTM. *See* Confederación de
  Trabajadores de México
Cuba, 32, 33, 55
Customs Law, 57
Customs valuation, 57
Czechoslovakia, 55

DDF. *See* Department of the
  Federal District
Debt
  international crisis, 32–33, 92–96
  private, 13, 21
  See also National debt
Decapitalization. *See* Capital flight
Deficits, 14, 16, 21–22, 23, 58–59.
  See also Government spending
Deflation, 16. *See also* Economy,
  contraction
de la Madrid Hurtado, Miguel, 10,
  14, 25, 27, 31, 32, 38, 40, 42,
  59, 63, 66, 68, 74, 77, 80, 90,
  92
Demand, 19, 23, 73, 74

Department of the Federal District (DDF), 77
Devaluation, 15, 19, 29. *See also* Fiscal policy
Development planning, 1, 38, 46
Development policies, 38, 47–48. *See also* Exports, promotion of; Import substitution
Domino theory, 32
Duties. *See* Antidumping duties; Countervailing duties

Echeverría Alvarez, Luís, 31
Economic Commission for Latin America (CEPAL), 98
Economy
  contraction, 12, 16, 69, 95, 98
  growth, 3, 9, 10, 11(table), 11–12, 15, 17, 22–24, 26, 34, 39, 87, 95, 96–97, 98
  policies, 11, 14, 19, 22, 88, 92
  See also Fiscal policy; Inflation; Oil, crisis
Ecuador, 92
Egypt, 25, 90, 92
Emigration, 11, 17, 24, 27, 38–39
Energy conservation, 75
European Community, 55
Exchange rates, 11, 12, 14–15, 16, 21, 22, 58, 64, 87–88, 93, 94, 96, 98
Exports, 14, 16, 19, 23, 52
  contraction of, 96
  credit and, 24
  energy. *See* Oil
  increase, 13(& table)
  promotion of, 38, 64, 88, 92, 96
  See also Oil, dependence on; Oil, international market; Trade

Federal Electricity Commission (CFE), 77
Financial market, 96, 105. *See also* Exchange rates
Fiscal policy, 12, 15–16, 23, 24, 38, 92. *See also* Economy, policies
Ford Motor Company, 46
Foreign Trade Law, 57
France, Boyd, 97
Fuel oil, 73
"Fuga, la." *See* Capital flight

Fundidora de Monterrey, 22

GATT. *See* General Agreement on Tariffs and Trade
General Agreement on Tariffs and Trade (GATT), 3, 20, 21, 22, 37, 38, 40, 41, 42, 43, 44, 48, 50, 51, 52, 55–59, 97
General Import Tariff Schedule, 57, 58
Gibbons, Sam, 43
Government spending, 14, 15, 21–22, 27. *See also* Deficits
Great Britain, 90
Gross domestic product, 2, 3, 14, 16, 69
Gross national product, 2
Growth, 3, 9, 10, 11(table), 11–12, 15, 17, 22–24, 26, 34, 39, 87, 95, 96–97, 98
GSP. *See* United States, Generalized System of Preferences

Heinz, John, 42
Hidalgo, Miguel, 69
Hydrocarbons. *See* Natural gas; Oil; Petrochemicals

IMF. *See* International Monetary Fund
Imports, 13(& table), 19, 26
  of inputs, 23. *See also* Petrochemicals
  oil economy and, 22
  restrictions, 38, 64, 69, 74
  See also Trade
Import substitution, 37, 45, 47, 75, 77, 79, 93–94, 98
Income
  distribution, 17
  per capita, 26
Independence. *See* Sovereignty; War of Independence
India, 48
Indonesia, 92
Industry
  development, 98
  incentives, 38
  privatization of, 12

protection of, 19–20, 38, 43–44,
64, 88, 96–98
Inflation, 2, 10, 11(& table), 15, 16,
23, 27, 28, 29, 69, 98
Institutionalized Revolutionary
party (PRI), 12, 29
Interest payments, 14, 18(table), 95
Interest rates, 21, 34, 68, 87, 93, 94
International Monetary Fund
(IMF), 9, 10, 11, 12, 14, 23,
26, 31, 94–95, 96
International Trade Court, 43
Investment, 23, 24
decline, 16
foreign, 12, 16, 21, 38, 39, 45, 59
incentives, 11, 16
performance, 38
state, 38
Iran, 83
Iraq, 83
Israel, 49

Japan, 41, 75, 88, 93, 97
Joint ventures, 39

Labor, 17, 23
organized, 28–29, 30, 31, 66, 80
petroleum, 66, 67, 68, 76–77, 80
U.S. workers and, 44, 45–46
Labor-Industry Coalition for
International Trade (LICIT),
45–46
LICIT. See Labor-Industry
Coalition for International
Trade
List of Products, 55
Living standards, 2, 11, 16, 23
Long, Russell, 43
López Portillo, José, 28, 31

Malaysia, 90, 92–93
Market incentives, 15
Martínez, Luís, 1
Mexican Petroleum Institute, 72,
75–76
MFN (most-favored-nation)
concept, 51, 52
Middle class, 29
Migration. See Emigration
Monetary reserves, 69
Monetary supply. See Fiscal policy

Monoexportation, 91–92. See also
Oil, dependence on
Moynihan, Daniel P., 42
MTN. See Multilateral Trade
Negotiations
Multilateralism, 42, 43, 48–49,
51–52
Multilateral Trade Negotiations
(MTN), 42, 43, 48

National debt, 2, 3, 9, 12, 15, 18(&
table), 20, 39, 93, 101–104
crisis, 9, 10–11, 24, 26–34, 42,
65, 91, 94
political stability and, 26–34
rescheduling, 14, 18, 24, 59,
68–69, 84, 94
servicing, 59, 87, 88, 92, 94–95
National Development Plan, 56
National Ecology Commission, 77
Nationalism, 1
Natural gas, 43, 56, 64, 67, 71, 72,
75
liquified, 73, 74
Natural resources, 56. See also
Natural gas; Oil
Nicaragua, 33, 55
Nigeria, 24
Nixon, Richard, 93
Norway, 83, 90
Nuevo PEMEX Petrochemicals
Complex, 74

OECD. See Organization for
Economic Cooperation and
Development
Oil
boom, 15, 27
crisis, 3, 9, 10, 11, 12, 14, 16, 20,
31, 68–70, 78, 87, 89–93, 94,
98
dependence on, 2, 3, 11, 22, 39,
64–65, 67–68, 76, 82, 91, 96
domestic trade, 73, 74–75, 79
exploration, 70–72, 79, 84
export limit, 56
export volumes, 72–73, 82–83
as financial instrument, 85–86
futures, 85, 90
international market, 75, 82–86,
89–90, 92, 95

marketing, 82–86
opportunity costs, 83
prices, 19, 22, 34, 42, 68, 74–75,
   78, 79–80, 82, 83, 84, 87, 90,
   92, 95, 96, 98, 106
production, 19, 67, 68, 70–71, 72,
   73–74, 84, 91
production costs, 79
refineries, 71
reserves, 3, 39, 72
sovereignty and, 63–68
Oil Expropriation Decree, 66
Oil industry
   nationalization of, 1, 63, 66, 69,
   70
   See also Petróleos Mexicanos
OPEC. *See* Organization of
   Petroleum Exporting Countries
Organization for Economic
   Cooperation and Development
   (OECD), 93
Organization of American States,
   58
Organization of Petroleum
   Exporting Countries (OPEC),
   19, 82–83, 90

PAN. *See* Partido de Acción
   Nacional
Partido de Acción Nacional (PAN),
   29
Patent protection, 40, 42
Paz, Octavio, 1
PEMEX. *See* Petróleos Mexicanos
Performance requirements, 46
Peru, 55
Peso
   crisis, 22
   overvaluation, 27, 58–59
   See also Exchange rates
Petrochemicals, 57, 73–75, 89,
   90–93
Petróleos Mexicanos (PEMEX), 2,
   3, 56, 57–58, 63, 64–65, 67,
   69, 70–72, 73, 74–81, 84–85,
   91, 99–100
Petrolization, 91
Philippines, 24
Plan Chiapas, 33
Planning. *See* Development
   planning

Poland, 55
Political economy, 1–6
Political stability, 24, 26–27, 28,
   32–33, 34
Political system, 26–34
Pollution, 77
Population, 17
PRI. *See* Institutionalized
   Revolutionary party
Prices, 11(table), 15, 16, 69. *See
   also* Inflation; Oil, prices
Private sector, 12, 18–19, 29–31
Privatization, 12, 21
Protectionism, 19–20, 38, 43–44,
   64, 88, 96–98. *See also* Trade
Protocol of Accession, 55–56, 57
Public sector, 11, 101–104. *See also*
   Government spending
Public Sector Commission on Rates
   and Prices, 79
Punta del Este talks, 48

Reagan, Ronald, 32, 41–42, 47
Reciprocity, 39, 40, 44, 46, 47, 52,
   58
Refineries, 71
Refugees, 33
Regulation, 15. *See also* Imports,
   restriction
Report of the Working Group, 55,
   56–57
Resource allocation, 15
Revolution (1910), 29, 69
Revolutionary Union of Oil
   Workers of the Mexican
   Republic, 80
Reynolds, Clark, 30

Saudi Arabia, 82, 83, 91
Savings, 16, 21
Serdan, Aquilles, 69
Silva Herzog, Jesus, 10, 94
Sovereignty, 1, 63–68, 84, 89, 92
Spain, 75
Special Committee for Consultation
   and Negotiation, 58
SPR. *See* Strategic Petroleum
   Reserve
Stability. *See* Political stability
Stabilization programs, 9, 10–11,
   12, 20–25, 31, 68, 95–96

Statists, 30
Strategic Petroleum Reserve (SPR),
  85
Subsidies, 17, 21, 38, 44, 48, 50.
  See also Industry, protection of
Sugar, 97–98

Tariffs, 19, 21, 48, 57, 58, 97. *See
  also* Protectionism
Taxes, 16, 21, 38, 92
Technology, 79
Trade, 12, 37
  adjustments, 13(& table)
  deterioration, 96–97
  disputes, 39, 41, 43, 45–46, 48,
    51
  economic growth and, 12
  negotiations, 42, 43, 48–52, 58,
    88–89
  policy, 37–46
  reforms, 21, 22
  sectoral agreements, 50
  surplus, 69
  terms of, 97
  with United States, 2, 18, 19–20,
    25, 37–54, 58, 59, 64, 75, 84,
    85, 88, 98

UNCTAD. *See* United Nations
  Conference for Trade and
  Development

Unemployment, 10, 12, 15, 17, 23,
  26, 27
United Kingdom, 83
United Nations Conference for
  Trade and Development
  (UNCTAD), 97
United States, 2, 14, 23, 29, 46–47,
  55, 93
  corporate interests, 44–46
  economic influence, 1, 10, 14, 16,
    18, 20, 22, 24–25, 34
  emigration to, 11, 17, 24, 27,
    38–39
  Generalized System of
    Preferences (GSP), 47, 52
  national security interests, 24–25
  trade with, 2, 18, 19–20, 25,
    37–54, 58, 59, 64, 75, 84, 85,
    88, 98
  Trade Act (1984), 47
  trade policy, 40–44, 47–53, 97
Uruguay, 46, 48
Uruguay Round, 46, 48, 49

Value maximization, 82–84
Velázquez, Fidel, 28, 66
Venezuela, 91, 93

Wages, 15, 28
War of Independence, 69
Worker's Confederation of Mexico,
  28, 66
World Bank, 12

Printed in the United States
by Baker & Taylor Publisher Services